THE
FINAL
THREE
✠✠✠
POPES

SIGNAL CHRIST'S RETURN

BY DR. JACK VAN IMPE

Printed in the United States.

Jack Van Impe Ministries
P.O. Box 7004, Troy, Michigan 48997

In Canada: Box 1717, Postal Station A
Windsor, Ontario N9A 6Y1

Website: www.jvim.com

ISBN 1-884137-55-5

✠
TABLE OF CONTENTS

✠
INTRODUCTION

Are we now living in the era of the final three Popes? Why do I believe these final three Popes signal Christ's imminent return?

I have read more than 12,000 volumes during my entire time of ministry, and I have over 100 Catholic volumes on my shelves — many of them have been a tremendous blessing to me. In preparing for this particular study, I chose 10 of the most important Catholic works.

1. The first is the Roman Catholic Douay version of the Holy Scriptures; this is the same as the King James Version. There is no difference in the teaching.
2. Next, The Catechism of the Catholic Church, with its 2,865 points — which I read twice, and was literally shocked with the teaching therein, because so many misrepresent what the Church really teaches!
3. The *Catholic Encyclopedia*, which totals many hundreds of pages in thickness.
4. A *New Catholic Commentary on Holy Scripture*, every verse from Genesis to Revelation.
5. *Crossing the Threshold of Hope* by His Holiness Pope John Paul II — and what a revelation this was. I'll be quoting from it a little later in this book.
6. Malachi Martin's *Keys of This Blood*. Here is one of the most intellectual Roman Catholic scholars ever to write a book, and he was a close friend of Pope John Paul II; he taught at the Pontificate Bible Institute in the Vatican.
7. *Raptured* is all about the pre-Trib Rapture as taught by Bishop Dougherty in some of the Catholic seminaries; and two of his students, Fathers Tombler and Funk, agreed exactly with what I believe about this subject.
8. Then *The Reign of Antichrist* by Father Culleton.
9. *Call of the Ages* by Thomas Petrisko.
10. *Hope of the Wicked* by the great Catholic leader Ted Flynn. These books helped me in what I'm about to write in this book: everything is documented. I want you to know exactly what the Catholic scholars said about a coming final Pope. This is going to be startling as I reveal these Catholic prophecies to you!

Yes, I am a Protestant — and I realize that sometimes Protestants tend to give a slant to their discussion of Catholic works. But what you are about to read is totally honest. In fact, I will go even further. I will prove that many times the Catholic Church has been *misrepresented* by Protestants who weren't completely honest in what they said about the Church's teachings. As I read through the 2,865 points of the Catholic Catechism, I had to change my mind about some of the things I've said in the past, because they were in error. As believers we must preach the truth in love; as Jesus said in John 8:32, "Ye shall know the truth and the truth shall make you free," and in these pages, you are going to read the truth.

CHAPTER 1
THE ANTICOMMUNIST

There was great happiness in Rome as they celebrated the 25th anniversary of Pope John Paul II's reign, when he was 83 years old. The headlines of the day paint an interesting picture: "Rome Diocese prepares spiritually for October the 16th." "Pope John Paul II leaves a lasting imprint as a world leader." "Will he be known as John Paul the Great?" While the Pope was visiting Toronto, Marcus Gee wrote a great article in the *Toronto Globe and Mail* describing why he thought John Paul was "great":

✠ He was the "repenting" Pope.

✠ He was the "healing" Pope.

✠ He was the "human rights" Pope because of bringing down Communism along with President Reagan.

✠ He was the "suffering" Pope who had arthritis, many surgeries, and Parkinson's disease.

Gee went on to say about the Pope, "As he suffered he continued to serve with joy. He was an everlasting and living example of everything he preached."

Why would a journalist call John Paul II the "repenting" Pope? Because John Paul went to Czechoslovakia and asked the Czechoslovakian Protestants to forgive the Catholic Church for putting some of their members to death in past centuries. He asked for forgiveness for St. Bartholomew's massacre of the Protestants in Paris, France, and also asked for forgiveness for putting Galileo to death because of disagreeing with the Church. When one asks forgiveness, this is the sign of a great man, and he was fulfilling what Jesus asked His people to do in Luke 24:47, when He said we are to preach repentance and remission of sins to all the world.

John Paul was also called the "healing" Pope. He tried to bring all Christians together in love. In John 17:21, Jesus is praying that we all might be one, that the world may believe that the Father sent the Son. Bickering, fussing, and fighting are not a healthy sign for Christendom. Ephesians 4, beginning with verse 3, says we believers are to endeavor "to keep the unity of the faith. For there is one body, one spirit, one

Lord, one faith, one baptism, one God and Father of all, who is above all, through all, and in you all."

John Paul was also the "human rights" Pope. He, along with President Reagan, brought down Communism. John Paul grew up in Poland — and the following figure shocked me: *Of the 6 million Jews that Hitler exterminated, 4 million of them died in Poland.* This Pope had a great love for the Jewish people. Many of his school buddies were Jews. In fact, the first visit to the Vatican by any human being during his reign was by his boyhood buddy, a Jew from Poland. John Paul not only fought Nazism, but also Communism, as he saw what this monstrous organization had done in his nation. He believed I Timothy 6:12 — that we are to fight the good fight of faith. And I'm sure when the rewards are passed out in the future for all of us at the Bema Seat, Pope John Paul II will be able to say, as did the Apostle Paul in II Timothy 4:7, "I have fought a good fight. I have finished my course, and I have kept the faith."

Journalist Gee also gave the Pope a great compliment by declaring that he was a living example of everything he preached. He had arthritis and Parkinson's disease and many surgeries, and there was even an attempt to take his life, yet this suffering Pope continued with joy. What a great example! One journalist said, as they saw the frailty of his body in his final days, "He is really a soul that's dragging the body from place to place."

There are five crowns, and one of them is given to those who suffer for Jesus. James 1:12 says, "Blessed is the man that endureth testing for when he is tried, he shall receive the crown of life." The Bible teaches that if we accept our suffering with praise, there's going to be a reward at the end of the trail. If we can say, "All things work together for good to them that love God, to them who are called according to his purpose" (Romans 8:28), then a special crown awaits those who suffered for our Lord.

What did Pope John Paul II believe and teach about the Five Fundamentals of the Faith?

✶ "Our mission," he said, "is to bear witness to Christ in the world."

✶ "Without conversion of heart," he said, "there is no personal peace."

✶ "Be converted to Christ." (He didn't say "to the Church," but "to Christ"!)

✠ "An intimate union with Christ is the secret."

✠ "Open your hearts to new life in Christ."

✠ "Christ is the Lamb who takes away sin."

✠ "The Son of man who gave his life as a ransom for sin."

✠ "Contemplate the Blood of Christ, the costly price of our freedom."

✠ He was also talking about the resurrection when he declared, "I know that my redeemer lives."

✠ "Enter with Christ into the joy of Resurrection."

✠ "The Church is the bride adorned for her husband."

✠ "Guided and assisted by the Holy Spirit, the Church lives in hope and awaits the coming of her bridegroom praying, 'Come, Lord Jesus.'"

He believed and taught all five points!

Later in this study, I will show you what the Catholic Catechism actually teaches about the return of the Lord Jesus Christ. Some priests need to get back into their catechism and see what is really taught there! I don't think they've kept up with the times, because this is the new revised catechism — by Cardinal Ratzinger, who became Pope Benedict XVI.

Another book was written by Pope John Paul II, *Crossing the Threshold of Hope*. I will quote from this book, and you will see that this man and his church have been misrepresented:

Page 9 — "Christ Himself is the Rock." That's not what we often hear.

Page 11 — "Christians are the bride of Christ" — that's when He returns at the Rapture.

Page 30 — he quotes Acts 4:12: "Neither is there salvation in any other for there's none other name under heaven given among men whereby we must be saved."

Pages 43, 111, 136 — "He is the one mediator between God and humanity."

Page 54 — he quotes John 3:16: "For God so loved the world that He gave His only begotten Son that whosoever believeth in Him should not perish, but have everlasting life."

Page 75 — "All believers, beginning with St. Paul have been lovers of the cross of Christ."

Page 80 — he quotes John 14:6: "I am the way, the truth, and the life. No man can come unto the Father, but by me."

I love this: On page 183 — "Preachers, priests, catechists, and Catholic teachers no longer have the courage to preach on hell." This reminds me of C. S. Lewis going to a Protestant service and encountering a young seminarian who didn't want to talk about hell, so he spoke about "eschatological consequences" — and of course "eschatology" has to do with latter-day things. So as he stood at the door, C. S. Lewis grabbed his hand and asked, "Young man, do you believe in hell?" "Yes, of course!" he replied. "Then why didn't you preach it," Lewis demanded, "instead of talking about eschatological consequences?" The Pope said likewise concerning Catholic priests who don't have the courage to preach the truth about eternal hell!

Proverbs 16:18 says, "Pride goeth before destruction and a haughty spirit before a fall." One of the sins God hates the most is *pride*. "These six things doth the Lord hate, yea seven are an abomination unto Him: A proud look, a lying tongue, hands that shed innocent blood, an heart that deviseth wicked imaginations, feet that be swift in running into mischief, a false witness that speaketh lies, and he that soweth discord among brethren." Number one on this list is *pride*. Satan was cast out of God's heaven because of pride. Proof? Isaiah 14:12-14: "How art thou fallen from heaven oh Lucifer, son of the morning? How art thou cut down to the ground which didst weaken the nations? For thou hast said in thy heart, 'I will ascend into heaven, I will exalt my throne above the stars of God, I will sit upon the mount of the congregation [God's throne] in the sides of the North. I will ascend above the heights of the heavens, I will be like the Most High God." Satan certainly had "eye" (I) problems. Jesus said in Luke 10:18, "I beheld Satan as lightning fall from heaven." I Timothy 3:6 lists the qualifications for ministers, stating that a minister is not to be a novice, a new convert. Why? Lest "being lifted up with pride, he fall into the condemnation of the devil," or literally into the same condemnation Satan fell into because of pride. The way up is down — and Pope John Paul II practiced humility as taught by his Savior. James 4:10: "Humble yourselves in the sight of the Lord and He shall lift you up."

Ali Agca, the Pope's would-be assassin, was visited in prison, and was blessed and forgiven, by Pope John Paul II himself. Certainly Pope

John's example teaches us much about forgiving others. But look at the opposite side: a shocking remark made by a pride-filled Marxist Jesuit who hated Pope John Paul II: "It's too bad Ali Agca couldn't aim straight." How shameful from a Jesuit Priest's lips!

Malachi Martin, an eminent theologian, expert on Roman Catholicism, and a professor at the Vatican's Pontifical Biblical Institute, wrote *The Keys of This Blood*. Martin quotes Pope John Paul II about the condition of the post-Christian Europe: "There's a vacuum in Europe, and there's no possibility that Christendom as it once was, will ever return to its original existence again." He is referencing the European Union, which began in 1948. I'm amazed as people write me saying, "When you talked about the European Council 15 years ago, I said, 'What in heaven's name is he talking about?' And now we see the EU — the European Union, its new name — in our headlines daily!" The first nations in the original Roman Empire were Belgium, Holland, and Luxemburg. Then in 1948, the revived Roman Empire started with the same three nations and was called Benelux. In 1957, Italy, France, and Germany joined for a total of six nations, and the union was ratified by the treaty of Rome. Again in 1973, Denmark, Ireland, and England joined for a total of nine nations. And finally in 1981, Greece became number 10. Centuries ago, Rabbi Hagion said that in the latter days there would rise a Gentile monarchy as a 10-division world empire, and when this event occurs, this would be the announcement that our Jewish Messiah would arrive. Irenaeus, the great church historian, in AD 140 said, "In the latter days just before Christ returns, there will be a 10-division world empire." One can find this in Daniel 7:7-8,20,24; Revelation 12:3; Revelation 13:1; Revelation 17:3,7,12,16. Get ready for a shock! One of the seven global organizations promoting a New World Order, the Club of Rome, has already created the plan and program for the World Empire. This is exceptionally exciting as we await Christ's return!

10-DIVISION WORLD EMPIRE

1. America, Canada, and Mexico	6. Japan
2. South America	7. South Asia
3. Australia and New Zealand	8. Central Asia
4. Western Europe	9. North Africa and the Middle East
5. Eastern Europe	10. The Remainder of Africa

The Holy Spirit has directed me to this new concept. I now see the One World Government as a 10-division World Empire ruling the globe, instead of just 10 nations.

Why are the members of the European Union opposing God or any reference to God in their new constitution? Because I John 2:18 says, "...Antichrist shall come," and there's a dual meaning here. "Antichrist" can mean "against Christ" or "substitute for Christ," and this is exactly what this global leader of the European Union, in the latter days, will do. He will speak blasphemies against Christ, according to Revelation 13:5 — and verse 6 adds that he will blaspheme the name of God and the name of the Lord Jesus Christ. He will proclaim himself as a deity, saying, "I am God!" That's not hard to imagine in this day of the New Age Movement, when millions are saying, "I am a little god and you are the God of all the little gods of the New Age Movement." Daniel 11:36: "He shall magnify himself above every god." Also, in II Thessalonians 2:4 we read that he will exalt himself above all that is called God or that is worshipped, so that he, as god, will sit in the temple of God, showing himself that he is God. The preparations are being made. The Antichrist is coming soon, and he will attempt to take the place of Christ. But his attempt will fail!

Two prominent men arise at that hour in history: the Antichrist and the False Prophet. The Antichrist comes out of the European Union — the political leader. But how will the religious leader — the False Prophet — work with the Antichrist? This religious leader will defect from the Christian faith. Revelation 13:11 pictures him as having the two horns of a lamb but speaking as a dragon. The two horns of a lamb identify him with the Christian faith, because Jesus was, and is, the Lamb of God that takes away the sin of the world (John 1:29), and Revelation 20:2 identifies the dragon with satanic power. So here is a Christian leader who defects from the faith and begins promoting this Antichrist, who hates God and hates the Lord Jesus Christ. The religious leader promotes the world leader to the point where he tells the public that they need to make an image of the Antichrist, and they do. Revelation 13:15 says, "The False Prophet has power to give life unto the image of this beast, that the image of the beast should both speak, and cause that as many as would not worship the image of the beast should be killed." This is not hard to believe either, in light of the many inventions that are now occurring in the world! He also does something else. Many centuries ago, Antiochus Epiphanes — some call him Antiochus Epimanes — the "mad one," went down to Jerusalem and put a pig on the altar in honor of the god Zeus; and this was called, in Daniel in 11:31 and 12:11, the "abomination that maketh [the Temple] desolate." Antiochus desecrated the Holy Temple in Jerusalem: Jesus mentioned the text I just quoted from Daniel, in Matthew 24:15 and Mark 13:14. He said, "When you see the abomination of desolation spoken of by Daniel the prophet, then let them which be in Judea flee to the mountains." He could not be talking about what Daniel was discussing in his day, because this is many centuries later. Thus Jesus said another time will come, similar to Daniel's day, when one will desecrate the Holy Temple of the Jews by setting up an image — and this is the hour mentioned in Revelation 13:15: The False Prophet has this image created in the likeness of the world dictator, and sets it up in the Jewish temple for worship. And by the way, it works! Revelation 13:8 says, "All that dwell upon the earth shall worship him whose names are not written in the book of life." Our Jesus is coming soon — because when this is all happening, the Lord Jesus Christ will return and destroy the Antichrist with the brightness of His coming (II Thessalonians 2:8). Later we find where He actually, and literally, casts this Antichrist and this False Prophet into the lake of fire (Revelation 19:20)!

The entire world was shocked and appalled by the sexual indiscretions of some Roman Catholic priests. This is what the Pope had to say about it: "Abuse by priests is a crime." A *US News and World Report* article reports the Pope as saying, "People need to know that there's no place in the priesthood and religious life for those who would harm the young.... We must be confident that this time of trial will bring a purification of the entire Catholic community, a purification that is urgently needed. So much pain, so much sorrow, must lead to a holier priesthood, a holier episcopate and a holier church."

The Pope took a real stand when these crimes were exposed in the United States and other places in the world. All of us should also take a stand, because Mark 9:42, speaking about little ones, states, "Whosoever shall offend one of these little ones that believe in me, it were better for him that a millstone were hanged around his neck and he were cast into the depths of the sea." God wants a holy people. I Peter 1:16 commands,

"Be you holy for I'm holy." II Thessalonians 4:7 says, "God hath not called us [Christians] unto uncleanness, but unto holiness." Hebrews 12:14 says, "Follow peace will all men and holiness, without which no man shall see the Lord."

In *Keys of This Blood*, Malachi Martin makes the Pope's feelings very, very evident. On page 79: "John Paul was aware, even as the ballot team went forward in the conclave that elected him, that highly placed churchmen, in and out of the Vatican, were fostering the inner decadence of Catholic faith and practice." On page 661: "There's been gross betrayal of the Roman Catholic church on an alarmingly high scale by priests and bishops." On page 676: "The desertion of Christ by the apostles, when Christ was arrested finds its mystical parallel in today's churchmen." Remember how they abandoned the Lord? Well, this is what he's talking about here: "They deny they know Him as the Son of God, or even that they know Him."

He was saying some of them are denying the way of salvation, or even that Christ is the way. Or even that Christ is God! Here's why: because we are approaching the last days just before Jesus returns. II Thessalonians 2:3 says, "Let no man deceive you for that day shall not come [Christ's return] except there come a falling away first." This is a falling away from the faith, called *Apostasia* in the Greek and *Apostasy* in English.

How bad is it going to get? I Timothy 4:1 says, "Now the Holy Spirit speaketh expressly that in the latter times some shall depart from the [Christian] faith, giving heed to seducing spirits and doctrines of demons, speaking lies in hypocrisy." It gets so bad that Revelation 9:20 warns multitudes will not repent of the works of their hands to cease from making and worshipping demons. What a day! It's here!

Will they deny that Christ is God in the final days? II Peter 2:1-2 says, "But there were false prophets among the people even as there shall be false teachers among you, who privily shall bring in damnable heresies, even denying the Lord that bought them, and bring upon themselves swift destruction. And many, many shall follow their pernicious ways, of whom the way of truth shall be spoken of in an evil way." It's here!

II Peter 3:3 says the doctrine they're going to mock the most is the return of Christ: "knowing this first, that there shall come in the last days scoffers saying, where is the promise of his coming? for since our fathers fell asleep all things continue as they were." But verse 10 says, "The day of the Lord will come." Jesus Christ will return! But that one little chapter in the book of Jude says that God-ordained ministers are to earnestly contend for the faith (Jude 1:3); and those who do not are called by God "filthy dreamers who defile the flesh" (Jude 1:8). There is a list of things there about these apostates who have drifted away that will startle you as you read this book of the Bible!

But they won't get away with it forever — because Jude 1:14 says, "The Lord cometh with ten thousands of his saints to execute judgment upon all, to convince all their ungodly among them, of all their ungodly deeds which they have ungodly spoken against him." Judgment day will come when Jesus returns!

This is not a reference only to Catholic priests, but to Protestant clergy as well — any ministers who deny what the Bible says about the Lord Jesus Christ being "the way, the truth, and the life" (John 14:6). In 1900, because of great liberalism among Protestants, we created a movement called "fundamentalism." They said, in essence, if you believe the five fundamentals of the faith, you are one of us. What are these five fundamentals?

(1) The virgin birth.
(2) The deity of Christ.
(3) The blood atonement of Christ upon the cross.
(4) The bodily resurrection.
And (5) His coming again.

Even today, there are many within Protestantism who mock these teachings. I'd hate to be in their shoes when our Lord returns, because when He does, He says to them who have rejected the true message, "Depart from me you cursed into everlasting fire prepared for the devil and his angels" (Matthew 25:41). He adds in verse 46, "These shall go away into everlasting punishment."

Pope John Paul II talked about old age as mentioned in Psalm 90:10: "The days of our years are threescore years and ten; and if by reason of strength they be fourscore years, yet is their strength labor and sorrow, for it is soon cut off and we fly away [into eternity]." A "score" is 20 years, so when he talks about threescore and 10, he's speaking about 70 years of age — fourscore is 80. But even if one reaches 80, it's soon over. Life passes by so quickly, and we need to be prepared. Job 7:1 says,

"Is there not an appointed time to man on the earth?" Hebrews 9:27 says, "It is appointed unto men once to die." The only way you can get out of this world is through death, or if the blessed Rapture happens in your lifetime. There's nothing we can do to stop death when that hour comes. Ecclesiastes 8:8 declares, "There is no man that hath power over his spirit to retain his spirit, neither hath he power in the day of death." But oh, when one is prepared, like the Pope said, it's "from life unto life"! I like this, because Titus 1:2 promises believers, "In guarantee of eternal life which God, who cannot lie promised." Pope John Paul II was trusting in that promise — as well as Philippians 1:21, "To die is gain."

II Corinthians 5:8 dogmatically states: "To be absent from the body is to be present with the Lord." This truth appears in the new updated catechism. *Absent from the body, present with the Lord — instantaneously.* This is why Revelation 14:13 says, "Happy are the dead who die in the Lord." The Pope also proclaimed, as you heard me say earlier, in his book *Crossing the Threshold of Hope,* that there is an eternal hell. Luke 16:23 adds, "The rich man died and was buried and in hell he lifted up his eyes being in torments." There are only two ways to go, heaven or hell (Matthew 7:13-14). Which way are you headed?

Catholics traditionally accept certain visions from various saints in the past. Saint Faustina Kowalska, regarding the Second Coming of the Lord Jesus Christ, predicted: "From Poland will come forth a spark that will prepare the world for Christ's second and final coming." Pope John Paul believed this prophecy, and described it as follows: "Humanity will see the Son of man coming in a cloud with power and great glory. This is the message which gives hope to the believer's heart." It's so near! Is there any doubt about it? Among Evangelicals, we have a group who believe in what is called "the Rapture" — but are there some in the Catholic Church who not only believe in the second coming of Christ to the earth, but also believe in the Rapture? Yes! We receive hundreds of letters from Roman Catholic people, many of them thanking me for showing such love for Pope John Paul II. I was sincere when I did so, because as I've shown you, he was a biblical scholar. Many of these Catholic people tell me that they heard about the Rapture when they were in grade school, so I know that some of the priests taught it. Fathers Tombler and Funk wrote a tremendous book on the Rapture, and I agree 100% with what they wrote. These priests learned about this great truth under Bishop Dougherty in a Catholic seminary.

Go back to Jerome's Latin Vulgate and look up I Thessalonians 4:16-18. Some say the term *rapture* cannot be found in the Bible. Is this so? The Catholic Latin Vulgate states: "The Lord Himself shall descend from heaven with a shout, with the voice of the archangel, with the trumpet of God and the dead in Christ shall be raised first. Then we which are alive and remain shall be *rapiemur* [yes, raptured] to meet the Lord in the air. So shall we ever be with the Lord."

Here is a typical letter among the hundreds I have received from Roman Catholic people who thank me for my love for them — this is from Robert and Lois Hockin. They were ecstatic as they wrote me because they found something extra-exciting about the Rapture. This teaching was by Archbishop MacEvilly, who did a tremendous work in 1898 as he explains the book of the Thessalonians verse by verse. Here's what he said (I couldn't have said it any better): "The order which shall take place in the resurrection, though instantaneous, is conceived in the following way: The Lord Jesus accompanied with all his angels, whom he shall command to be ready, will descend from heaven. He shall issue his command to the archangel, who with a loud voice, like that of a trumpet, shall sound the signal of the resurrection. At this sound, all the dead shall arise, and those alive shall be changed — all the just shall be caught up [*rapiemur*, raptured] into the air to meet the Lord while the reprobate shall be at his left hand, and left behind, on the earth."

The circumstances are fully recorded in I Corinthians 15:51-54. What does it say? "Behold, I show you a mystery. We shall not all sleep [all be dead] but we shall all be changed [dead and living] in a moment, in the twinkling of an eye at the last trump: for the trumpet shall sound and the dead shall be raised incorruptible and we the living shall be changed. For this corruptible [the dead], must put on incorruption and this mortal [the living] must put on immortality." When it happens, we'll be able to victoriously cry out in that day, "Oh death, where is thy sting — oh grave, where is thy victory?"

But I want you to notice something. This text says, "I show you a mystery." A mystery in the Bible is something that *has not been taught until this point of time*. You cannot find it in the Old Testament; you cannot find it in the four Gospels. Why? Christ only taught about His coming to earth. But the mystery of the Rapture was the truth hidden, and *only revealed to the Apostle Paul*. It's impossible to mistake what he is teaching. The dead will rise incorruptible and the living shall be changed. If it's just a resurrection of the dead and nothing happens to the living, as far as being raised or raptured, living believers would be cheated. It would be better to be dead when one hears the words "Come up hither," so all the dead and living believers could all be there. But one does not have to be confused — because the dead rise first, then we which are alive and remain shall be caught up (*rapiemur*) with the dead to meet the Lord in the air!

When the Pope's health was failing, there was great speculation as to who would succeed him. "Experts ponder papal succession," the headlines read, and "Cardinals discretely look for a new Pope." There was a group of people in Rome looking to become the new Pope. "Front row scramble to film the Pope's demise, and become the one who would succeed him — it was called the war of the terraces."

Now I'm going to take you all the way back to 1226 and Francis of Assisi. He made a great prediction: "There will be an uncanonically elected Pope who will cause a great schism. There will be divers thoughts preached which will cause many, even those in the different orders to doubt, yea, even agree with heretics, which will cause my order to divide. Then there will be universal dissensions and persecutions."

Imagine, St. Francis of Assisi hundreds of years ago saying that the last Pope would defect from the Christian faith! I find that this is classified in Catholic theology under "tradition." Even Bishop Sheen proclaimed this truth. This is powerful!

After the Darkness states, on page 328: "There will come a time of hard trials for the church. Cardinals will be against cardinals and bishops against bishops. Satan will put himself in their midst. In Rome, also there will be big changes. What is rotten will fall, and what will fall must not be maintained. The church will be darkened and the world plunged into confusion." This agrees exactly with what the Bible teaches. At the end time, there will be a religious leader who will depart from the faith.

I have been quoting Catholic sources, Francis of Assisi and others, who say there will be a final Pope who will defect from the faith, and they foresee the rivalry that exists now between cardinals, bishops, priests — the infighting goes on, there's no doubt about it. The Catholic leaders are saying it themselves. But now prepare to be shocked by a prophecy of St. Malachy — a prophecy that Pope John Paul II believed.

We will cover it briefly here and go into more detail in Chapter 7.

In 1139, in Tuam, Ireland, there was an archbishop by the name of Malachi O. Morgair. Later, because he was canonized, he was known as St. Malachi. (Don't confuse this with the Malachi Martin we have been discussing.) This was St. Malachi in 1139, who had just been to Rome. God showed him what was coming in the future, that there would be numerous popes, from Pope Cellestine II onward, who would reign for approximately 800 years, and then there would be two more Popes following Pope John Paul II.

Now St. Malachi gave poetic descriptions of every one of the Popes, and the shocking thing is, he's been right. I totally accept this prophecy because of four outstanding Catholic leaders — I will present them chronologically:

First, Francis of Assisi predicted that the final Pope would defect from the faith.

Secondly, Bishop Sheen believed it, and promoted it on national television in America.

Thirdly, Malachi Martin assured us in his writings, *The Keys of This Blood*.

Fourthly, Pope John Paul II knew this was coming from the day he entered the position as Pope. He saw the defection and he knew what the second secret of Fatima was — that there would be this great apostatizing among the clergy, bishops, cardinals, etc. Since Pope John Paul II figured that the prophecy would be true, he did everything possible to keep it from happening in the next choosing of a Pope, when the white smoke would flow. So, before his decease, he chose 31 new cardinals. There are only 190 total Cardinals, and 185 had been chosen by Pope John Paul II; only five were not. All these men guaranteed when they voted that there would be one more conservative Pope. This would be Pope Benedict XVI, who would faithfully preach God's Word as it is. Then the final Pope would reign — and he would bring grievous error into the Catholic Church and faith. He would also reign during the Battle of Armageddon.

Remember: the Battle of Armageddon is when the Lord Jesus Christ returns to stop history's most devastating battle (Revelation 11:18). Now let's look at some information from Malachi Martin's book. Page 684: "At that time Roman Catholics will then have the spectacle of a pope validly elected who cuts the entire visible body of the church loose from the traditional unity and the papacy oriented apostolic structure that the church has hitherto always believed and taught was divinely established. The shudder that will shake the Roman Catholic body in that day will be the shudder of its death and agony, for its pains will be from within itself orchestrated by its leaders and its members. No outside enemy will have brought this about. Many will accept the new regime, many will resist. All will be fragmented. There will be no one on earth to hold the fractionating members of the visible Roman Catholic body together as a living compact organization. Men will then be able to ask for the first time in the history of the church, 'Where is the visible body of the church Christ founded?' But there will be none."

It seems unbelievable, and yet, there is great hope because the Bible teaches that the Lord is coming back to stop all the confusion and all of the apostasy on the earth, and put an end to Armageddon. He is going to bring peace on earth for 1,000 years (Revelation 20:4).

Let me give you a little historical background for what I'm about to write in conclusion. The rabbis of old taught that Messiah would come and rule on earth for 1,000 years. Rabbi Akibba, Rabbi Bechai, Rabbi Eliezer, Rabbi Elias, and many others based this teaching on the Word of God. They said God created the world in six days (Genesis 1:31) and rested on the seventh day (Genesis 2:2). And since a day is like 1,000 years (Psalm 90:4 and II Peter 3:8), these texts mean that this world will go on for six days, represented by the six days of creation, or 6,000 years, for a day is like a thousand years. Then our Lord Jesus will come and reign for 1,000 years (the seventh day).

The Catholic Church believed this because of II Peter 3:8: a day is like a thousand years, and a thousand years is like a day. So they said, like the rabbis, history will go on for 6,000 years and then our Savior, the Lord Jesus Christ, will come. The Tribulation period and Armageddon will conclude 6,000 years of history, and then we enter the final day, the thousand-year reign of Christ on the earth. *We are approximately at that hour of history now.* Because of multiplied calendars with various dates, including that of Judaism, we know the blessed event of Christ's return is near, even at the door, but we know not the day or the hour (Matthew 24:33,36).

How do we know that the Catholic Church originally taught this? Because the Council of Nicea meeting in the year AD 325 witnessed the gathering of 318 bishops of the Catholic Church. They came from every corner of the world, gathering in Rome to reaffirm the thousand-year reign of Christ — the Millennium. The teaching was divinely passed and accepted.

But something happened in AD 431. There was a man by the name of Origen, and Pope John Paul II in his book *Crossing the Threshold of Hope* says he was one of the first heretics within the Church. He taught universalism, stating there is no such place as hell because everyone will be saved. He and his friend Ambrose both hated the Jews; they said since these Jews are teaching that their Messiah is coming for a thousand years, let's get this error out of Christianity. So at the Council of Ephesus in AD 431, everything changed. At this Council it was agreed that there would be no thousand-year reign of Christ. This error is called *Amillennialism*, meaning no millennium. This damnable teaching went entirely against scores of verses in God's Word. Imagine: it was an anti-Semitic move, but it worked. It infiltrated Catholicism and Protestantism. It wasn't long until the critics and haters of the Jews said everything vile about God's chosen people (Deuteronomy 7:7-8) in an attempt to rid any decent statement about the Jews from God's Word.

They began to manipulate God's Holy book by translating symbolically, or allegorically, the word "Israel" as "the Church" 2,604 times, and "Jerusalem" as "heaven" 813 times. A total of 3,417 times, these two terms were blasphemously changed. When the priests during the Protestant Reformation left the Church, they took this teaching with them — which is why Protestantism today is inundated with this erroneous teaching: that there will be no Rapture or thousand-year reign of Christ. Instead, they taught that at Christ's return, the world ends. This erroneous teaching was called Replacement Theology.

Was I thrilled when *Reuters News Service* reported that Pope John Paul II, before his decease, said, "The world will never end!" This was code language meaning that he was going back to Catholicism's roots. So what does the Catholic Church teach about the Second Coming of Jesus Christ? I implore all Amillennialists in Protestantism and Catholicism who don't believe there will be a thousand-year reign of Christ on earth to consider the newly edited Catholic Catechism. Let me show you exactly where this great truth about Christ's Return is found — so you could even look it up for yourself in the Catechism:

✶ Point 840 discusses the coming of the risen Messiah.

✶ Point 2816 — The Kingdom of God lies ahead of us —

in Christ we shall reign.

✴ Point 2818 — In the Lord's prayer, "thy kingdom come" refers primarily to the final coming of the reign of God through Christ's return to earth.

✴ Point 2817 — The petition is "maranatha" — the cry of the spirit and bride — meaning come Lord Jesus. Indeed, as soon as possible, Lord, may your kingdom come, and thy will be done on earth as it is in heaven when the King comes — Matthew 6:10.

✴ Now this really sends chills up my spine: Point 349 — The Eighth day begins the new creation. Now, if one believes in the eighth day, they must believe in the seventh day, the Millennium! No doubt about it.

✴ But there's more! After the 1,000 years, which was the seventh day, Christ is re-commissioned (I Corinthians 15:24-28). This is the beginning of the eighth day, which constitutes the eternal reign of Christ upon the earth. You cannot mistake it. I repeat: this eighth day begins eternity on earth, because heaven has been transferred from the third heaven of II Corinthians 12:2 to earth, not only for the 1,000 years, but forever and ever and ever.

And I could quote more verses — 120 of them — that the earth will never cease to be.

There are two words in the Greek in the New Testament dealing with the "end of the world" error. The words are "Neos" and "Kainos." *Neos* means a new creation. *Kainos* means a remodeling job. Every time the Bible speaks about the new heaven and the new earth, it is Kainos — a remodeling job. The Roman Catholic Catechism agrees with what I've been preaching for 65 years. Yes, the eighth day begins the new creation, but what does this mean?

The Catholic Catechism — Point 1042 — The universe itself will be renewed, not recreated. This is plain enough, isn't it? Point 1047 — the visible universe then is itself destined to be transformed, renewed, and restored to its original state. Amen and amen! But this is the most important fact I am going to share with Preterists and manipulators of the Word of God concerning Replacement Theology. They state that God is through with the Jews forever, and therefore you have changed God's Word 2,604 times, saying that Israel is the Church. However,

Point 765 in the Catholic Catechism states, "The twelve tribes of Israel become the foundation stones of the New Jerusalem." See Revelation 21 and 22. And the eighth day begins the new and eternal creation (Point 349).

Every sign is in place. Soon Jesus Christ will come and set up His kingdom. Heaven will be on earth forever and forever, and the world will never end. This is why the monks every day in their monasteries pray using this terminology — as everyone does as Mass ends: "World without end, Amen and amen." This is God's Word, in Isaiah 45:17 and Ephesians 3:21: "Now unto God be glory in the church by Christ Jesus throughout all ages, world without end."

Do you want to be a part of all that's about to happen and be with Jesus forever like Pope John Paul II proclaimed? Remember that Titus 1:2 says it's a guarantee that God, who cannot lie, promises to those who receive His Son. Will you do it this moment?

Pray this prayer: *Father, thank you for sending Your son Jesus to die on the cross for my sins. I want to be ready when He comes to rule and reign here on earth. I want to be with You forever, Lord Jesus, so I invite You to come into my heart. Save me! Wash away every sin through that precious blood You shed upon the cross. I accept Your sacrifice at Calvary this day for my sins. In Jesus' name, Amen.*

(If you just prayed this prayer, write to me and I'll send you absolutely free our booklet, "First Steps in a New Direction." This material will help you grow spiritually and fulfill II Peter 3:18: "But grow in grace and in the knowledge of our Lord and Savior Jesus Christ. To Him be glory both now and forever. Amen.")

✠
CHAPTER 2
LIBERATION THEOLOGY

Dr. Malachi Martin was a Jesuit in the Society of Jesus for a number of years. When he saw the drift of the Jesuit organization to Marxism, Leninism, he made his significant departure to remain with the brand of Catholicism to which he had always been devoted.

He taught at the Vatican's Bible Institute and indoctrinated many of today's priests, bishops, and cardinals.

He became one of the most prolific Catholic theologians producing numerous 600-page books — *The Jesuits, Hostage to the Devil, The Final Conclave, The Decline and Fall of the Roman Church, The Encounter, The Vatican,* and others.

I have read a number of his great books and especially loved his two masterpieces, *The Keys of His Blood* and *The Jesuits.*

This compilation of excerpted facts will bless you as much as it has inspired me. Jesus said: "You will know the truth and the truth will set you free." See for yourself:

Malachi Martin's great book, *The Jesuits: The Society of Jesus and the Betrayal of the Roman Catholic Church,* includes these revealing passages:

Looking at the Society of Jesus from the outside, at the time of Teilhard de Chardin's death in 1955, anyone would surely have been struck by the signs of its flourishing vigor, from its still-growing membership to its ever-spreading influence in the wide world.

On the inside, however, was the brute fact that the Jesuit "sense of mission" was that the Church could not much longer be satisfied within traditional molds in its long and mostly covert struggle with the hierarchic Church of Rome.[i]

In the wake of Teilhard's stunning work of the 1920s and in the quasi-respectable tradition of French Liberal Catholicism, along came another Frenchman in the 1930s — Catholic philosopher Jacques Maritain ... Maritain adopted a sort of theology of history, as one might call it, built on Marxist philosophy.[ii]

Next arose another Dominican, Father Congar....

For him, every step of temporal progress in the secular world, every people who liberated themselves from domination by the right wing or by capitalists, represented a step in the development of the kingdom of God. The Church must become the universal sacrament of the new cosmic salvation being ushered into man's *Liberation Theology*.[iii] Almost before it had a name, however, it spread like fire, setting alight the minds of many, first of all in Latin America, but quickly then rushing through Asia, India, South Korea, Taiwan, and sub-Saharan Africa. It had invaded theological seminaries in the United States and Europe by the early 1970s. Very soon, even political lobbies joined the chorus in contented harmony[iv] *declaring* freedom from Rome's theology and participation with the "People of God" in the interest of social evolution and revolution encased in the term liberation *built on a misapprehension of Marxism....*

For Marx, the historic task of the proletariat was to struggle against the capitalists and to liberate the people from their oppression....[v]

The "preferential option for the poor," for example, as Guiterrez and others explained it, was based on Christ's own preference for the poor, his preference for the working class verses the rich ... wasn't it easier for a camel to slip through the tiny eye of a needle than for a rich man — a capitalist — to get into heaven? And remember Lazarus, the disease-ridden hobo of Christ's own parable of salvation? And Dives, the fat capitalist of the same parable? Which of these two finally rested in the bosom of Abraham and which was tortured on the tip of hell's flames?[vi]

And on and on it continued.

For each and every Catholic term about piety, belief, asceticism, and theology, it was taken over by Liberation Theologians.

The refinement of such co-opted terms permits grinning twists and ugly distortions of Roman Catholicism, as when the Marxist Junta of Nicaragua calls its mobs of bully boys "las turbas divinas," the divine mobs.[vii]

Soon Liberation Theology — freedom from the little Caesars of Rome with their abstract formulas, judicial rulings, traditional hierarchy, and freedom to join in changing the fundamental structure of man's society — was adopted by the Jesuits.

....Once Jesuits admitted the attitude that all prior theology was only speculation, and useless speculation at that, as far as Latin America was concerned, all need to study Thomism and traditional Scholastic Theology and philosophy in Jesuit seminaries ceased. An immediate consequence was that budding priests and theologians in the Society of Jesus were put at two removes from the teaching, language, tradition, and pieties of the Church.

First, all traditional textbooks, manuals, doctrinal treatises, and other instruments of the "old theology" were judged to be out of date, and were to be jettisoned. Standard textbooks about moral rules and problems, as well as recognized authorities on the theology of the Church and on biblical matters, all were abandoned — indeed sometimes were throw out or burned.

Second, because "the people" were not the source of "theology," Jesuits began to step back from the traditional hierarchy of the Church. Vow or no, what could loyalty to the papacy and its prerogatives possibly mean any longer? As Jesuit Fernando Cardenal put it, his priesthood would have lost its meaning if he did not resist the commands of the Pope and stay on as a member of Nicaragua's Marxist Junta.

The rise and development of Liberation Theology, and the extraordinarily sympathetic response of the clergy — and notably of the Jesuits — presented the Roman Catholic Church with a painful and costly loss not only in the so-called Third World of undeveloped countries, but in the First World of developed countries as well.

....The latter-day conversion of Jesuits — indeed of the Society of Jesus — to Liberation Theology means that Rome had lost the services of the one organization that should have provided it with a solution to the Catholic Church's problem in Third World countries.[viii]

....The Society ... used the Council to justify its 180-degree turn from its mission as a team of papal defenders and propagators of the official Roman Catholic doctrine into an organization bent on altering the face of traditional Roman Catholicism and, inevitably, the political complexion of many nations.[ix]

Let's investigate — Father General Kolvenbach, the Pope of the Jesuit organization, stood in the struggle between John Paul II on the one side and Fernando Cardenal with his Liberation Theology colleagues throughout Latin America on the other. The occasion was a document issued under John Paul's authority by Joseph Cardinal Ratzinger, head of the Vatican's powerful Congregation for the Doctrine of Faith (CDF), the Roman Ministry charged with overseeing the purity of Catholic teaching. The CDF document criticized Liberation Theology and its practitioners for their adoption of the Marxist analysis of history, and for their insistence on the "class struggle" and the proletarian [poor working class] revolution as integral parts of genuine Christianity. Between the lines of the document despite Stato's prior warnings was the implicit rejection of Soviet Marxism-Leninism.[x]

Casaroli [Secretary of State for the Jesuits] had an eye on his friends at the other side of the Iron Curtain who had excoriated the Ratzinger document as "the disgrace of our time." The Secretary wished to tell those friends that … he had told the Pontiff, he intended to nurture and protect his lines of communication with Moscow and its eastern European satellites; that meant tender treatment of Marxism and its modern womb, the Soviet Union.[xi]

….As Secretary of State, he would have to place a distance between himself and Ratzinger's documents….[xii]

The signs became more ominous for the Modernists — Jesuits and non-Jesuits — when Ratzinger gave a long interview to an Italian journalist-writer, and then published the interview as a book. Ratzinger's point: Since Vatican II, and because of false interpretation of its documents, there was not one area of Church belief and morality that had not been corrupted.[xiii]

The new doctrine of Liberation Theology according to Segundo, a Jesuit leader and author, was a defense of every Jesuit priest who shouldered a carbine and joined the jungle guerillas. It made it clear why Jesuits could be ministers with portfolio in Marxist governments; why Jesuits attacked John Paul II acridly for his teaching on sexual morality; why Jesuits spent their days and their lives solving union problems, organizing sugarcane workers, running factories, constructing low-cost housing, helping the Planned Parenthood Federation of America spread the use of contraceptives, run nationwide hospital and dispensary networks, organize political demonstrations for this and against that, accordingly as the issues of the day were presented by the "teaching authority" of the "people's Church [Jesuits]." These are the actions of the new faith, true to the new theology according to which the material needs of men must be the prior object of the Church's efforts.[xiv]

Really? I always thought the purpose of the Church was to preach the Gospel — "And he said unto them, Go ye into all the world, and preach the gospel to every creature" (Mark 16:15). And what is that Gospel? "Moreover, brethren, I declare unto you the gospel which I preached unto you, which also ye have received, and wherein ye stand; For I delivered unto you first of all that which I also received, how that Christ died for our sins according to the scriptures; And that he was buried, and that he rose again the third day according to the scriptures" (I Corinthians 15:1,3,4). This great eternal scriptural demand is what the present Jesuits call useless speculation. Perhaps the rich capitalists they condemn in this report to an eternal hell they'll share with the Marxist Communists.

✠
CHAPTER 3
THE GREAT APOSTASY
II THESSALONIANS 2:1-17

The following is taken from another of Malachi Martin's scholarly works, *The Keys of This Blood: Pope John Paul II Versus Russia and the West for Control of The New World Order:*

"The parallel between the betrayal of Jesus as a living, tangible man by Judas and the betrayal of the Church by the members of the anti-Church instills a horror in the believer, while enlightening him as to the reality of the danger in which the Roman Catholic institutional organization was caught in the 20th century."[xv]

If the secular reaction to Pope John Paul II in the early days of his reign was strewn with misunderstanding, concern, and confusion, it has to be said that most of those within the Roman Catholic Church itself were still more astonished and baffled.

Here, however, the consternation centered around the bare fact, visible to everyone everywhere, that John Paul's Church was in shambles....[xvi]

For the faithful in his Church, and arguably for the millions who had left it in pain and dismay during the long pontificate of Pope Paul VI, John Paul was more than an ordinary public figure, more than a man, more even than a religious leader. For them, he had become the personal representative of God on earth. His was the ultimate voice of authority about how the world should be governed by men. He was the court of last resort for all human doubts. He was supposed to fix the Church. Or at least to run it.

For those who treasured the amber-encased papacy that John Paul had already put behind him forever, it was too much by far to see a Pope who allowed himself to be touched and greeted and addressed, and yes, even rebutted by millions of ordinary men and women. That he had already been appropriated in some sense by millions of very different people, baptized and unbaptized, and that he obviously intended to travel the world in order to continue that overdemocratic process, shattered the fragile mold within which large numbers were convinced the papacy — the real and Catholic papacy — must ever remain.[xvii]

At this point while the Jesuit movement was becoming Marxist in philosophy believing they could do all things without Christ. Pope John Paul II shocked the apostates within Catholicism.

In a 24,000-word document known, as papal documents generally are, by its now famous first words, <u>Redemptor Hominis,</u> John Paul displayed a depth of thought and consideration coupled with a message that was characteristically simple and startling.

No human activity escapes the religious dimension, he said; but especially important are the activities that constitute the sociopolitical life of men and women wherever they reside. Indeed, the note that dominated and animated that encyclical document was John Paul's insistence that the hard, intractable problems of the world — hunger, violation of human dignity and human rights, war and violence, economic oppression, political persecution — any and all of these can be solved only by acceptance and implementation of the message of Christ's revelation announced by the papacy and the Roman Catholic Church.

With the delivery of that encyclical, Pope John Paul seemed to mark a turning point....[xviii]

Milwaukee's Archbishop Rembert Weakland, arguably no stranger to notorious behavior, stepped far beyond the normal bounds of public comment for high Churchmen characterized John Paul II as "a ham actor whose speeches don't make sense unless you dramatize them."[xix]

As his intimate associates knew, John Paul was aware, name by name and to his own pain, of Churchmen with front-rank power over the sinews of Church strength who were committed to his failure as defender of the Church and its traditional moral and religious teachings, and as defender of Petrine authority itself....

It seemed to take no time at all, for example, for an increasing and remarkably vocal array of cardinals, bishops, prominent theologians, and laypeople everywhere to join forces openly, as a phalanx of in-Church adversaries to John Paul and his authority. Aptly dubbed the anti-Church, this widely dispersed group was recognized by John Paul — as well as by his advisers and his adversaries — as conscious and willing collaborators of all who saw the Church, its papacy, and its independent centralized governing structure as an unsuitable and ill-fitting element of modern life.

Then as now, John Paul understood that these anti-Church elements within his Church were reckoned publicly as Catholics. Then as now, however, and as John Paul understood equally well, these same anti-Church Churchmen saw every new announcement of the fledgling Pope — his every break with tradition, his every innovation, and, above all, his encyclical letter The Redeemer of Men — as an unacceptable obstacle to the personal leadership roles they fancied for themselves on the highroad of humanity toward its near-future destiny as a world society[xx] of Marxist Jesuits.

The purpose and the agenda of this superforce were clear enough to John Paul. But what about the motive? What was this superforce after, should its adherents be successful in their hostile takeover attempt? And aside from the fact that many of them were cardinals, bishops, priests, prominent theologians, and influential Catholic laypeople, what characterized the members of this superforce?

According to those who even then opposed it as best they could on a daily basis, the partisans of this anti-Church-within-the-Church were, for the most part, as they are today: individuals who had for a variety of reasons exchanged their Catholic faith for another, more to their liking.

More serious than that, however, was the fact that a certain number among them — and virtually all of these were, as they are today, in ecclesiastically high places — had thrown their weight on the side of those outside the Roman Church who recognized in the papacy, and in the centralized governing structure beneath it, the global force that stood then as now between today and all the tomorrows of a brave new world.

The heart and essence of the struggle between John Paul and the superforce was clear to both sides. It concerned, then as today, the building of a new and global society whose outlines were even then emerging. The superforce consisted of visionaries who, along with John Paul's adversaries in the secular world outside the Church, had long since thrown themselves into a tug-of-war for control of that global society.[xxi]

ENTER POPE JOHN XXIII

In the fall of 1958, the smiling, rotund little Cardinal of

Bergamesque peasant stock, Angelo Giuseppe Roncalli, was elected to the papacy as John XXIII. Within a scant three months of his election, Pope John XXIII stunned his Catholic hierarchy and the entire world with the announcement that he would convene the 21st ecumenical council in the 2,000-year history of the Catholic Church. The Second Vatican Council.

With that announcement came a sort of undeclared truce in the deep and professional enmity long held by the Vatican and the Church against Marxism and the Soviet Union. For all the decades since Lenin's coup d'état of 1917 and right through the papacy of Pope Pius XII, the Soviet Union and its Marxism were considered and described as the enemy of Catholicism and the seedbed of anti-Christ.

During the three years of preparation for the Council that followed his initial announcement, however, Pope John XXIII reversed that policy for the first time. For one of his principal aims was to convince Nikita Khrushchev to allow two Russian Orthodox clerics from the USSR to attend his Council in Rome as observers.

....At Khrushchev's insistence, the Pontiff secretly agreed that his upcoming Council would not issue a condemnation of Marxism and the Communist state.

Such an agreement was a huge papal concession; for precisely such condemnations had always been included as standard fare in any Vatican or Roman Catholic commentary on the world at large. And the scope of Vatican II, as the Council was quickly dubbed, was certainly intended to include the world at large.

Another price Pope John paid came as a deep disappointment to millions of faithful and expectant Catholics around the world, and came to be seen by them as another breach in the Catholic anti-Communist rampart. A powerful Church tradition had it that if, in the year 1960, the reigning Pope would perform a public act consecrating the Soviet Union to the protection of the Virgin Mary, the USSR would be converted from its official hard-core atheism, and a long period of world peace would ensue.

As it turned out, John XXIII was that Pope. But in the circumstances, he felt that to carry out such a public act would be to declare war all over again on Khrushchev's Soviet Union, branding it anew, and on an international stage, as a nest of atheists. "This step is not for our time." Pope John XXIII observed privately, and he shelved the whole proposition.[xxii]

In time, as was only logical, Buddhists, Shintoists, animists, and a host of other non-Christian and even non-religious groups would find a place in the poorly and broadly defined new "ecumenism."

In such various ways — sometimes open, sometimes very subtle indeed — was the breach steadily widened in what had for so long been the Catholic bulwark against Communism.[xxiii]

ENTER POPE PAUL VI

As reigning Pope, Paul VI gave a farewell address to the departing bishops of the Council on December 5. That speech provided the broad philosophic and quasi-theological umbrella beneath which secularism within the Roman Church would be protected from the storm of protest and outrage mounted by traditional Catholics in the years following the Council.

While the Catholic faithful were protesting, that same speech was used by the heirs of Antonio Gramsci, a leading communist, to drive a coach-and-four as handsomely as you please through the worldwide structural organization of the Roman Catholic Church.

Pope Paul VI told the departing bishops that their Church had decided to opt for man; to serve man, to help him build his home on this earth. Man with his ideas and his aims, man with his hopes and his fears, man in his difficulties and sufferings — that was the centerpiece of the Church's interest, said the Pontiff to his bishops.

So pointedly did the Pope elaborate on that theme of the Church's devotion to subserve material human interests that Gramsci himself could not have written a better papal script for the secularization of Roman Catholic institutions or for the de-Catholicization of the Roman Catholic hierarchy, clergy, and faithful.

By the mid-1960s, then — with Brezhnev at the helm of the Leninist geopolitical structure and with Paul VI at the helm of the Roman Catholic georeligious structure — it appeared that the ghost of Antonio Gramsci had all but won the day. In Moscow, his doctrine of revolution through disguised and clandestine penetration of capitalist populations had come out on top in the political wars of the Leninist-Marxist leadership.[xxiv] *And in Rome, the Second Vatican Council had handed over so ...swiftly that the linchpins of Vatican and papal control were* replaced by the action-oriented demands of the new theology. The most powerful religious orders of the Roman Church — Jesuits, Dominicans, Franciscans. Maryknollers — all committed themselves to Liberation Theology. In Rome and in the worldwide field of their apostolates, the policies and the actions of these religious orders became the lifeblood of the rising colossus of Liberation Theology.[xxv]

Corruption of the best is the worst corruption. It was not long before a majority of diocesan bishops — not only in Latin America but in Europe and the United States as well — were swept up in the new theology of this worldly liberation. The entire effort was helped along by the careful and intricate networking of Catholic dioceses by a new creation: the Base Community. Essentially composed of lay Catholics, each Base Community decided how to pray, what priests to accept, what bishops — if any — would have authority, what sort of liturgy they would tolerate. All reference to traditional Catholic theology and to Rome's central authority was considered secondary, if not altogether superfluous.

The Base Communities in Latin America — riddled with Liberation Theology and openly Marxist in their political philosophy — were pronounced in their hatred of the United States. They were stubborn in their attachment to the Soviet Union. And they were fierce in their preference for violent revolution — the one non-Gramscian note in an otherwise faithful adherence to his blueprint.

The accelerating spread of both Liberation Theology and Base Communities was boosted beyond measure by several factors. But among the most important was the string of Peace and Justice Commissions — branch offices, as one might say, of the central Commission in Rome — that existed throughout the worldwide dioceses of the Roman Church. These commissions became powerful allies of Liberation Theology. Manned mostly by clerics, nuns, and laity who were already convinced Marxists, they turned themselves into centers for the dissemination of the new theology. They ate up Vatican funds to pay for congresses, conventions, bureaucratic trips, and a flood of printed materials — all of it aimed squarely at the reeducation of the faithful.[xxvi]

Christian-Marxist dialogues and conventions were everywhere. The influence of the unequivocally Marxist and pro-Soviet World Council of Churches went through the roof. Traditional principles of education collapsed in Catholic schools, from primary through university levels.

The refusal of Western bishops to insist on obedience of the faithful to Church laws about divorce, abortion, contraception, and homosexuality became the norm, not the exception. Everywhere, in fact, there was a massive lethal thrust, on Antonio Gramsci's terms, at the Catholic and Christian culture of the Western nations.

By the time John Paul II came to the papacy, in fact, it was no longer even a secret that echelons of clerics in the Vatican itself had been deeply affected. Indeed, perhaps the profoundest victory of the Gramscian process was visible primarily in the mind-boggling confusion, ambiguity, and fluidity that was already the hallmark of Rome's reaction to the rapid de-Catholicizing of the Church, as well as of Vatican dealings with bishops who sometimes openly declared their independence from papal authority. To a large degree, papal and Vatican control had been effectively removed from the georeligious machinery of the Roman Catholic Church.

Pope John Paul did not arrive from Poland unaware. He understood better than most what had happened to his Church in the West. He was, in fact, probably the only major non-communist world leader who knew the contribution Antonio Gramsci had made to operational Marxism around the world, and who understood both the murky process he had advocated and the Leninist machinery in which that process was now enshrined.

Nevertheless, if John Paul had hoped that in his five papal trips to Latin America he could put a dent in the allegiance of his clergy there to Liberation Theology, or that he could recall his bishops and his religious orders in the region to their vows of obedience, he was disappointed in those hopes. No papal exhortations in public or in private, and no directives by his Vatican, made the slightest substantial difference in the situation there.

Indeed, by 1987, the pro-Soviet and violence-prone Base Communities in Latin America alone numbered over 600,000. By comparison, there were not even 1,000 Roman Catholic dioceses in North and South America combined — and virtually all of those were at least questionable in allegiance to Rome.[xxvii]

Pope John Paul II rejected the Marxist Leninist Communism practiced by the Jesuits, Dominicans, Franciscan, and Maryknollers. They became committed to Liberation Theology.

While Americans, even in the late 20th century, were still trying to make up their minds as to whether "a nation so conceived and so dedicated can long endure," their contemporary Transnationalists and Internationalists had decided that the greatest sociopolitical venture ever devised by man — the new world order — could indeed long endure.

John Paul's summary judgment about the Grand Design of Transnationalists and Internationalists was perforce negative. The design could not succeed, according to him, but must and would end in catastrophe. He had two main reasons for this judgment.

The design is built on the presumption that we ourselves are the authors of our destiny. Man is exalted. The God-Man is repudiated; and with him, the idea of man's fallenness is rejected. Evil is a matter of malfunctioning structures, not in any real way a basic inclination of man. Behind the godless and un-Christian design of Transnationalists and Internationalists there stands man as a Nietzschean figure, a Superman. If it were so, in the age of Superman there would no longer be any reason to believe in Christian morality, individual liberty, and equality before the law. Attachment to civil rights, to the dignity and welfare and political worth of the individual, would become illusory and pointless.

Superman replaces the God-Man, Jesus Christ — a Superman as man-god. Culture loses its very heart, which is religion, with its worship of the divine and its observance of God's laws against human-originated evil. Thereby politics as a function of culture loses its equilibrium because it has lost the source of its human decency. G. K. Chesterson was correct when he asserted that when man ceases to believe in God, most likely man will believe in nothing.

John Paul's second reason — the more cogent one for him, personally — is drawn from the Fatima message. That message predicts that a catastrophic change will shortly shatter any plans or designs that men may have established. This is the era of the Fatima "or" the time when men have abandoned religion. God does not intend to let human affairs go on for a long time in that fashion, because this is His world — he created it for His glory, He made it possible for all men to attain the heaven of His glory, by sending His only son, Jesus Christ, to expiate the punishment due men for their sins.

This is why John Paul waited. God must first intervene, before John Paul's major ministry to all men could start.[xxviii]

POPE JOHN PAUL II'S STAND AGAINST MARXISM, LENINIST COMMUNISM

Europe was beyond the reach of re-Christianization by the normal means. Reform of his Church could not be achieved by the customary ecclesiastical means. He tackled neither.

What is difficult for many to understand is his reason for not tackling those problems head-on. The reason is, as should be expected, geopolitical. That is difficult enough for many of his contemporaries, for the simple reason that few people think geopolitically or understand such implications. An added layer of difficulty is added by the distinctly Polish and Roman Catholic character of John Paul's geopolitical outlook.

For nearly two centuries, Catholic Poles were denied all participation in national politics. The Polish nation did not exist; the Polish people existed as a function of other nations, and their fortunes were tied to geopolitical factors. Besides, as a nation, Poles had — literally for centuries — identified their national politics with the georeligion of Roman Catholicism....

And no wonder! Poland was held prisoner by the most organized totalitarian power the world had ever known, cast off and unaided by the only other political powers — in the West — that could have helped her. Poland had successfully confronted that Soviet power; confronted it, struggled with it, and finally defeated it, becoming, as Adam Michnik said, the laboratory for the other Soviet satellite nations, none of which had been able to deal with Leninist Marxism except in total submission.[xxix]

The result of choosing Marxism over John Paul's rejection of the Jesuits and other Catholic group's apostasies is that "throughout every region and in every department of Roman Catholic life today there is an inescapable and continuous slippage into disorder, disunity, confusion, unfaith, and open apostasy. It is a rampant decadence everywhere, sparing nobody and no elements — seminaries, diocesan and Roman chanceries, religious orders, male and female, schools, colleges, universities, families, our liturgy, our theology, our morality, our devotions, our missions in Africa and Asia, our personal standards. Everything about us has been affected by this slippage."[xxx]

Where will this apostasy within Catholicism take the global Church of Rome? Malachi Martin's book on page 684 talks about the time when this Pope who defects reigns. At that time ... "Roman Catholics will then have the spectacle of a pope validly elected who cuts the entire visible body of the church loose from the traditional unity and the papacy oriented apostolic structure that the church has hitherto always believed and taught was divinely established. The shudder that will shake the Roman Catholic body in that day will be the shudder of its death and agony, for its pains will be from within itself orchestrated by its leaders and its members. No outside enemy will have brought this about. Many will accept the new regime, many will resist. All will be fragmented. There will be no one on earth to hold the fractionating members of the visible Roman Catholic body together as a living compact organization. Men will then be able to ask for the first time in the history of the church, 'Where is the visible body of the church Christ founded?' But there will be none visible." [xxxi]

✠
CHAPTER 4
ONE WORLD GOVERNMENT, THE NEW WORLD ORDER AND GLOBAL RELIGION, AND THE ARRIVAL OF CHRIST'S KINGDOM UPON EARTH

God's Word delivers a powerful truth about the latter days you must not miss!

> Daniel 2:1-13:
> And in the second year of the reign of Nebuchadnezzar, Nebuchadnezzar dreamed dreams, wherewith his spirit was troubled, and his sleep brake from him.
> Then the king commanded to call the magicians, and the astrologers, and the sorcerers, and the Chaldeans, for to show the king his dreams. So they came and stood before the king.
> And the king said unto them, I have dreamed a dream, and my spirit was troubled to know the dream.
> Then spake the Chaldeans to the king of Syriac, O king, live for ever: tell thy servants the dream, and we will show the interpretation.
> The king answered and said to the Chaldeans, The thing is gone from me: if ye will not make known unto me the dream, with the interpretation thereof, ye shall be cut in pieces, and your houses shall be made a dunghill.
> But if ye show the dream, and the interpretation thereof, ye shall receive of me gifts and rewards and great honour: therefore show me the dream, and the interpretation thereof.
> They answered again and said, Let the king tell his servants the dream, and we will show the interpretation of it.
> The king answered and said, I know of certainty that ye

would gain the time, because ye see the thing is gone
from me.
But if ye will not make known unto me the dream, there
is but one decree for you: for ye have prepared lying
and corrupt words to speak before me, till the time be
changed: therefore tell me the dream, and I shall know
that ye can show me the interpretation thereof.
The Chaldeans answered before the king, and said,
There is not a man upon the earth that can show the
king's matter: therefore there is no king, lord, nor ruler,
that asked such things at any magician, or astrologer,
or Chaldean.
And it is a rare thing that the king requireth, and there is
none other that can show it before the king, except the
gods, whose dwelling is not with flesh.
For this cause the king was angry and very furious, and
commanded to destroy all the wise men of Babylon.
And the decree went forth that the wise men should be
slain; and they sought Daniel and his fellows to be slain.

Perhaps at some time in your life you've had a dream that was so
unnerving and perplexing that it kept you from sleeping through the rest
of the night. You tried to figure out what it might mean and may have
even asked others to help you with an interpretation that made sense.
If this has happened to you and me, we know it's happened to people
throughout history.

In the year 603 BC, King Nebuchadnezzar had a dream so
bizarre that he marshaled his wisest men to his chambers to give
him a reasonable interpretation. Not only did the crafty king want an
interpretation of the dream he could understand, but he went one step
further: He demanded a recital of the dream itself. Unreasonable? Of
course. But Nebuchadnezzar was the king, and just as the gorilla sleeps
anywhere it likes in the jungle, so the king could make up his own rules
— which he did with an impish look in his eye, I'm sure.

NERVOUS COUGHS AND FURTIVE LOOKS

Did the king really forget the content of his dream? I doubt it. I think this was Nebuchadnezzar's way to test the wisdom and alleged supernatural powers of his magicians, astrologers, and sorcerers. Heavy has been the head that has worn the crown throughout history, and Nebuchadnezzar's crown must have weighed a ton. Kings come and go; their enemies are forever nipping at their heels. What if Nebuchadnezzar's dream were to portend evil for his realm? Superstitious as he was, he demanded an interpretation.

But there was a risk that one of the palace sorcerers might give the king information he didn't want to hear. So what does a wizard do? Equivocate? Beat around the bush? Try to buy some time? After all, the wrong information would produce disastrous results for the wizards — like being cut to pieces and having their houses made into a dunghill. But if they could state the dream and give Nebuchadnezzar an interpretation he could live with, then all manner of blessings would fall on the necromancers. So the stage was set.

I can almost hear the nervous coughs and see the furtive looks as one magician after the other would say something like, "Oh King, that's a marvelous idea, our telling you your dream — not that it will be easy. Say, would you mind running that dream by your servants just one more time? And then I'm sure we'll be able to come up with just the right interpretation."

PARANOIA ABOUNDS

The king didn't bite. He knew he had his magicians and wise men trapped, and he accused them of stalling. Finally, probably with perspiration pouring from their brows, the wizards and astrologers came flat out with the truth, saying that such an assignment was impossible — certainly too great a job for the wisest person in the realm, and one that could only be accomplished in cooperation with the gods — whose "dwelling is not with flesh" (Daniel 2:11). An interesting comment from savants who were supposed to be able to predict the future and come up with detailed — and accurate — answers to life's most perplexing problems. Yet, when push came to shove, they figured hearkening to the gods might not be such a bad idea after all.

But the king didn't buy their delay and became furious. In a fit of rage he demanded that all the wise men of Babylon be rounded up and destroyed — something we've seen again and again throughout secular and religious history. When frustration mounts in the palace, scapegoats are found, and these innocents are often summarily done away with. It happened when a paranoid King Herod, intent on finding an alleged usurper to his throne, put out a decree to kill all Jewish baby boys in the land. We saw it with Hitler who, in his cruel attempt to create his Third Reich, killed six million Jews, burned all books that threatened his reign, and more than decimated all non-Aryans under his control. We saw it again just a few years ago, in the mid-to-late 1960s, when an equally paranoid Chairman Mao threw all of China into convulsions with his demented "Cultural Revolution" — a nationwide witch hunt that was only an official excuse to kill and maim millions of dissidents, destroy any semblance of ancient tradition that flew in the face of his hybrid communism, and put China on a crash course with history. Will tyrants ever learn?

Now, the net was thrown wide throughout the kingdom of Nebuchadnezzar to bring all the men of wisdom to their knees and ultimately to their collective death. Although it appears that Daniel and his friends were not in this shouting session with the king, they were, in fact, to be included in the king's order. The great irony of the king's manifesto as it related to Daniel was that once again God was setting the stage for a display of His sovereignty over the affairs of men. Meanwhile, the hunt was on.

> Daniel 2:14-24:
> Then Daniel answered with counsel and wisdom to Arioch the captain of the king's guard, which was gone forth to slay the wise men of Babylon:
> He answered and said to Arioch the king's captain, Why is the decree so hasty from the king? Then Arioch made the thing known to Daniel.
> Then Daniel went in, and desired of the king that he would give him time, and that he would shew the king the interpretation.
> Then Daniel went to his house, and made the thing known to Hananiah, Mishael, and Azariah, his

companions:

That they would desire mercies of the God of heaven concerning this secret; that Daniel and his fellows should not perish with the rest of the wise men of Babylon.

Then was the secret revealed unto Daniel in a night vision. Then Daniel blessed the God of heaven.

Daniel answered and said, Blessed be the name of God for ever and ever: for wisdom and might are his:

And he changeth the times and the seasons: he removeth kings, and setteth up kings: he giveth wisdom unto the wise, and knowledge to them that know understanding:

He revealeth the deep and secret things: he knoweth what is in the darkness, and the light dwelleth with him. I thank thee, and praise thee, O thou God of my fathers, who hast given me wisdom and might, and hast made known unto me now what we desired of thee: for thou hast now made known unto us the king's matter.

Therefore Daniel went in unto Arioch, whom the king had ordained to destroy the wise men of Babylon: he went and said thus unto him; Destroy not the wise men of Babylon: bring me in before the king, and I will shew unto the king the interpretation.

DANIEL'S STRATEGY

We've now begun to see the sterling character of Daniel. Though still young, he was wise beyond his years; though relatively inexperienced in the affairs of life, he demonstrated how God can use a servant who gives his absolute loyalty to the Father. Now, it was again Daniel's turn to settle uncontrollable waters. Here's where we as believers need to take careful note of Daniel's spiritual strategy. First, he asked for time — always a good idea when we are trying to come up with a solution to one of life's challenges. Second, he was bold enough to say that he would fulfill the king's demand — that is, he promised to do what the other wise men could not. Daniel knew that with God on his side he was not stepping out on a partially sawed-off limb. He knew his heavenly Father would give him the insight required at the time he would need it. Third — and how often we fail to do this — Daniel went back to his quarters and held an impromptu prayer meeting/counseling session with his companions Hananiah, Mishael, and Azariah. Proverbs 15:22 reminds us, "Without counsel purposes are disappointed: but in the multitude of counselors they are established." Daniel knew the importance of feedback from his companions — an awareness that runs throughout the entire book.

DANIEL'S "MODEL PRAYER"

Now I want you to pay special attention to Daniel's prayer — just one of the many prayers of this great man of God we will discover in the pages of this amazing prophecy. Remember, Daniel already believed that God would give him the answer he'd need when he would soon stand before the king. He'd already conferred with his friends and received their counsel. But Daniel knew that unless he prayed earnestly to his God for divine insight and wisdom, he would never be prepared for his daunting assignment with a paranoid king.

For years, I've felt this prayer of Daniel should be a model for our own time with God — a prayer that moves me anew as I read it again, perhaps for the thousandth time. Daniel blesses God for His wisdom. He acknowledges that earthly kings are just that — as common as dirt — and that God alone sets up rulers and brings them crashing down from their man-made thrones. He recognizes that only His God — not Marduk, or any other Babylonian idol — gives wisdom to the wise and has the necessary resources to bring light to that which is shrouded in darkness. Then, in a final burst of praise, Daniel thanks God for the wisdom and might He's given to His servant. Daniel thanks God — giving no credit to himself — for the answers he now has to King Nebuchadnezzar's dream. Can't you just hear Daniel's prayer build with confidence as he moves toward his final crescendo — his glorious amen to his God?

READY TO MEET THE KING

Daniel has done his homework. He's been patient. He's prayed. Now he's ready with an exuberance and confidence that can only come to a believer in the one true God. Only after this serious, pre-audience preparation does Daniel finally say to Arioch, "All right, now's the time. I'm ready to enter the presence of the king ... and by the way, make sure that the king spares the lives of the wise men of Babylon. There's now no reason for them to die."

Daniel, a young man with limited life experience, is now used by God to shape the destiny of an entire kingdom.

The apostle Paul, hundreds of years later, would say to another young man, Timothy, "Let no man despise thy youth; but be thou an example of the believers, in word, in conversation, in charity, in spirit, in faith, in purity" (1 Timothy 4:12). In God's eyes, age has little significance when it comes to being a wise servant. Just as He did then, all God demands from His people is obedience. This spirit would be the hallmark of the man Daniel to the end of his days.

> Daniel 2:25-30:
> Then Arioch brought in Daniel before the king in haste, and said thus unto him, I have found a man of the captives of Judah, that will make known unto the king the interpretation.
> The king answered and said to Daniel, whose name was Belteshazzar, Art thou able to make known unto me the dream which I have seen, and the interpretation thereof?
> Daniel answered in the presence of the king, and said, The secret which the king hath demanded cannot the wise men, the astrologers, the magicians, the soothsayers, shew unto the king;
> But there is a God in heaven that revealeth secrets, and maketh known to the king Nebuchadnezzar what shall be in the latter days. Thy dream, and the visions of thy head upon thy bed, are these;
> As for thee, O king, thy thoughts came into thy mind upon thy bed, what should come to pass hereafter: and he that revealeth secrets maketh known to thee what shall come to pass.
> But as for me, this secret is not revealed to me for any wisdom that I have more than any living, but for their

sakes that shall make known the interpretation to the
king, and that thou mightest know the thoughts of
thy heart.

GLORY TO GOD ALONE

Daniel now had the king's attention. He also continued to remind
the king that the wisdom he was sharing was from the one true God and
not from his own knowledge. What integrity! Daniel could have made
this a public relations spectacular for himself by taking all the credit,
comparing himself to the other wise men (who failed to speak the dream
or interpret it), saying, "Hey, King, look at me. I'm the man. You can
always count on me for the answers to your tough questions."

But that is not the Daniel of this book. He took no glory for himself,
but instead insisted that only God in heaven could do what the king had
requested. I can almost see King Nebuchadnezzar's mouth begin to drop
as Daniel set him up. Nebuchadnezzar was probably saying something
like, "Come on, Daniel, enough of this 'My God' stuff. What's my
dream? More importantly, what does it mean? And why are you making
me wait?" But Daniel was not to be rushed. He was in control of this
particular discussion, and, once again, the king was compelled to wait
for the time when this young Jew would come forth with his secrets,
which he finally shared when he said (Daniel 2:31-36):

> Thou, O king, sawest, and behold a great image. This
> great image, whose brightness was excellent, stood
> before thee; and the form thereof was terrible.
> This image's head was of fine gold, his breast and his
> arms of silver, his belly and his thighs of brass,
> His legs of iron, his feet part of iron and part of clay.
> Thou sawest till that a stone was cut out without hands,
> which smote the image upon his feet that were of iron
> and clay, and brake them to pieces.
> Then was the iron, the clay, the brass, the silver, and
> the gold, broken to pieces together, and became like
> the chaff of the summer threshingfloors; and the wind
> carried them away, that no place was found for them:
> and the stone that smote the image became a great

mountain, and filled the whole earth.
This is the dream; and we will tell the interpretation
thereof before the king.

I imagine the king was startled, and dumfounded, probably
exclaiming something like, "I can't believe this, Daniel. You're a genius!
You've done what my most seasoned astrologers and magicians could not
do. You're amazing ... and you're still so young!"

Daniel just stood there and listened politely, continuing to assert that
God gave him the dream. He probably reminded the king of what he'd
already told him, "But there is a God in heaven that revealeth secrets"
(2:28). Wouldn't you like to have seen Nebuchadnezzar's face as Daniel
spoke the dream one scene at a time? The king's heart rate must have
increased as Daniel talked about an image so large and brilliant that
it was virtually impossible to look at for any length of time. His blood
pressure must have climbed as Daniel described the statue from head
to foot — the head of gold; breast and arms of silver; belly and thighs
of brass; legs of iron; and feet and toes of an unstable mixture of iron
and clay.

THE DREAM INTERPRETED

Then, thundering from a distance came a stone cut out without
hands — that is, not of human origin — crashing into the statue with
such meteoric force that it dissolved the image into chaff, blowing away
any semblance of the statue. Where the image had stood — this is
what had to give King Nebuchadnezzar pause — the stone, now a large
mountain, "filled the whole earth" (2:35). If you were a superstitious
Babylonian king constantly looking over your shoulder at the slightest
movement of your enemies — or wondering if inside-the-palace
intrigue might one day do you in — what would you think if you had a
dream like this? Without waiting for the king's response — or perhaps
because Nebuchadnezzar was too dumbfounded to respond — Daniel
proceeded with the interpretation of his dream.

Daniel 2:36-45:
This is the dream; and we will tell the interpretation
thereof before the king.

Thou, O king, art a king of kings: for the God of heaven hath given thee a kingdom, power, and strength, and glory.

And wheresoever the children of men dwell, the beasts of the field and the fowls of the heaven hath he given into thine hand, and hath made thee ruler over them all. Thou art this head of gold.

And after thee shall arise another kingdom inferior to thee, and another third kingdom of brass, which shall bear rule over all the earth.

And the fourth kingdom shall be strong as iron: forasmuch as iron breaketh in pieces and subdueth all things: and as iron that breaketh all these, shall it break in pieces and bruise.

And whereas thou sawest the feet and toes, part of potters' clay, and part of iron, the kingdom shall be divided; but there shall be in it of the strength of the iron, forasmuch as thou sawest the iron mixed with miry clay.

And as the toes of the feet were part of iron, and part of clay, so the kingdom shall be partly strong, and partly broken.

And whereas thou sawest iron mixed with miry clay, they shall mingle themselves with the seed of men: but they shall not cleave one to another, even as iron is not mixed with clay.

And in the days of these kings shall the God of heaven set up a kingdom, which shall never be destroyed: and the kingdom shall not be left to other people, but it shall break in pieces and consume all these kingdoms, and it shall stand for ever.

Forasmuch as thou sawest that the stone was cut out of the mountain without hands, and that it brake in pieces the iron, the brass, the clay, the silver, and the gold; the great God hath made known to the king what shall come to pass hereafter: and the dream is certain, and the interpretation thereof sure.

NOT SO FAST, O KING

Daniel was anything but timid, for God had removed any spirit of fear from his heart as he stood eye-to-eye with Nebuchadnezzar, giving him the message from God. Nebuchadnezzar undoubtedly saw himself as a self-made king — powerful, in control, able to make heads roll at a snap of his finger. Yet Daniel says, "Wait a minute, King. Not so fast. You are only where you are because my God has given you dominion, power, and glory. Yes, you're a mighty and powerful king, but your reign simply cannot last." Daniel consistently gives God the credit in the preface of all his prayers and speeches. The king would probably rather not have to sit there and listen to these extended preambles, but this was young Daniel's moment. And Nebuchadnezzar would have to be patient.

Daniel's description of Babylon's place in world history is fully in sync with other historical references. Babylon was the greatest power of the day. It had always been a superlative empire, with its great beauty, economic position as a center of commerce, and fabled hanging gardens — one of the exquisite wonders of the ancient world. But even all these accomplishments, Daniel would argue, were not Nebuchadnezzar's doing — but God's. Although Nebuchadnezzar was the "gold head" in his dream, the inference was that he would not be in charge of his kingdom in perpetuity: Daniel's message was that God was in control, and that his heavenly Father would have the final say as to who would and who would not occupy all earthly thrones — including Nebuchadnezzar's.

KINGDOMS COME ... KINGDOMS GO

Marduk, Babylon's chief god, was also called the "god of gold" — something that surely did not escape the king's notice. In fact, the precious metal gold was almost synonymous with the nation of Babylon. There was gold everywhere — in the ornate palaces, the worship places, and the ubiquitous shrines. Even the walls were overlaid with what was then the most precious substance in existence. Now King Nebuchadnezzar was told that all this gold would one day be swept away by a second kingdom, the kingdom of Medo-Persia.

This later became a historic fact when the two disparate cultures — the Medes and the Persians — united in 550 BC under one king to form a great world power. This was the "silver" part of the statue and a proper representation of the Medo- Persian empire since the Medes and Persians based their partnership on the power of money collected through an elaborate system of taxation. Nebuchadnezzar must have been relieved to hear Daniel prophesy that this "silver" kingdom would be inferior to his own, probably because as a partner nation, Medo-Persia did not have the political and military unity of Babylon. But despite this weakness, Medo- Persia would one day break the "head of gold." Because God's Word speaks only the truth, we should not be surprised to note that Daniel's prophecy became reality when Medo-Persia brought Babylon to its knees in military defeat in 539 BC.

But what about the third kingdom, the belly and thighs of brass? The element bronze later became a characterization of the Greek empire, primarily because the Greeks used it extensively as the material for their weapons of war. Daniel foresaw that Greece would one day "bear rule over all the earth" (2:39). History shows that Greece did dominate the world of its day. Alexander the Great's kingdom encompassed much more of the known world than Babylon or Medo-Persia ever did. Again, a prophecy of Daniel was fulfilled in world history.

THE RENEWAL OF THE ROMAN EMPIRE

Imagine how Nebuchadnezzar must have reacted to the news from this young prophet. His was probably a mixture of fear and disbelief. But we must also note that Daniel wasn't finished yet, and the king did not interrupt Daniel's interpretation.

After the world-dominating empire of bronze, another empire would arise — a fourth kingdom composed of two legs of iron. This kingdom would be Rome with its "two legs" representing the expansive empires of the Western Roman Empire, headquartered in Rome, and the Eastern Roman Empire, with the cosmopolitan city of Constantinople as its capital. This empire also would fall. The great historian Edward Gibbon powerfully describes it in his work entitled *The Decline and Fall of the Roman Empire*. However, just before Christ returns, this empire will revive as the iron mixed with clay begins to wiggle in the form of 10 toes.

Only God could have given Daniel the wisdom to know what is now becoming reality for us who live in the latter days of the 20th century.

According to Daniel, the final revival of the Roman Empire would be comprised of a 10-division empire, which would finally lead to a new world order encompassing the globe. Why would they come together? For monetary and military security and strength — something we're already seeing as the European Union moves ahead with such plans at break-neck speed. Thus, Nebuchadnezzar's image with 10 toes pictured the revival and conclusion of the Roman Empire.

Note the gradual deterioration of the metals in Nebuchadnezzar's dream: from gold to silver to bronze to iron to clay, a clear demonstration that as history marches on, men and their cultures become increasingly corrupt. Tregelles is a scholar who has called attention to the decreasing "specific gravity" of each of these metals. For example, the specific gravity of gold is 19; silver, 11; brass, 8.5; cast iron, 7.8; mixture of iron and clay, 1.93. The world in which you and I live — the world of the fourth and revived fifth kingdoms as prophesied by Daniel — is going to get worse up to the moment that the great stone breaks the feet of the image. That stone is Jesus Christ, who becomes a mountain and fills the entire earth. "And in the day of these kings shall the God of heaven set up a kingdom, which shall never be destroyed: and the kingdom shall not be left to other people, but it shall break in pieces and consume all these kingdoms, and it shall stand for ever" (2:44).

THE 10 TOES BEGIN TO WIGGLE

The entire end-time message is predicted here in the Book of Daniel thousands of years, in some instances, before the actual historical events occurred — just as Rabbi Shvili in 1935 suggested in his book, *Reckonings of Redemption*. How could Daniel know this? Because God, historically, has chosen to reveal His secrets through Spirit-anointed prophets.

Let's bring Daniel's prophecy even closer to home. There was a long interval between the time when Rome's power began to wane and fall — around 476 AD — and the year 1947 when the 10 toes of the statue began to wiggle. First of all, Benelux met in that year — Belgium, the Netherlands, and Luxembourg — creating the first three members of the confederation. In 1957, three additional nations met with the countries of Benelux — Italy, France, and Germany — for a total of six, ratified by the Treaty of Rome. Little by little, in our daily newspapers, we see a revival of the Roman Empire just as Daniel predicted. In 1973, England, Ireland, and Denmark joined the confederation, making it a total of nine members. Then, on New Year's Day, 1981, Greece became number 10. These nations of the EU now number 27 and will soon be joined by Islamic nations as predicted by Martin Luther and John Calvin and they together will rule the New World Order, a 10-division global empire and one world religion. The time that Daniel prophesied is here. We are living in the latter days, and Jesus is coming soon.

JESUS IS OUR ROCK

One of the most profound messages of these verses is that you and I don't have to worry about straightening out our world. We have almighty God, Adonai, who is in charge of the affairs of earth. Jesus is the rock, that stone, on which the true Church is built. You'll remember in Matthew that Jesus asked the apostle Peter, "Whom do men say that I am?" Peter answered, "You are the Christ, the Son of God." And Jesus said, "On this rock I will build my church" (see 16:13- 18). Christ was that rock (1 Corinthians 10:4). Yes, the rock in Nebuchadnezzar's dream that eventually engulfs the entire world, a rock that will hit the feet, not the head — Babylon; not the chest and arms of silver — the Medes and the Persians; not the stomach and thighs of brass — Greece; not the legs of iron — Rome. They went out of existence. Instead, the rock strikes that group that revives at the time of the end — the 10 toes, the restored Roman Empire. Thus, on January 1, 1981, when Greece became number 10, pictured by the 10 toes on the image, we were given the clearest signal yet that we were headed toward the last days and would soon be ushered into an environment that would be ready for the return of Christ as King of Kings and Lord of Lords (Revelation 19:16).

GOD'S SOVEREIGNTY

We can therefore reasonably conclude that the dream of Daniel Chapter 2 reveals that the kingdom of God will soon be established in connection with the second coming of our Savior. Daniel 2:44 states, and I repeat this for the sake of emphasis, "And in the days of these kings shall the God of heaven set up a kingdom, which shall never be destroyed: and the kingdom shall not be left to other people, but it shall break in pieces and consume all these kingdoms, and it shall stand for ever." It's all starting to happen. Just as the image in Nebuchadnezzar's dream contained metals that degraded as they descended from gold to iron and clay, so will the world in which you and I live become increasingly apostate and the more our society at large will be governed by outright militarism as its only vehicle to control the violence that is present and that is yet to come.

What was the actual purpose of Nebuchadnezzar's dream? To show God's sovereign rule over the affairs of men, leading to the future Gentile world domination and its ultimate destruction, to be replaced by a Kingdom and a King who would reign forever on earth (Matthew 6:10).

One of the reasons the Book of Daniel is so important is that it provides us with a complete scenario for the end of the age. And it all begins to wind down with the current revival of the Roman Empire, which I believe is the present-day European Union. After this episode is completed, there is no more. This will be the last empire, and it will continue into the latter days, with the Antichrist as the primary figure taking over the resurrected Roman Empire (Revelation 17:10). He will be a dictator of world proportions and will rule the world of his day just as King Nebuchadnezzar ruled his world as leader of Babylon. But for those of us who know the whole story, we need not fear the perilous times yet to come, because "the stone [which] was cut out of the mountain without hands" (2:45) is none other than the person of Jesus Christ, God's anointed, our Savior, the Rock of our salvation. When He returns to gather His own, God will establish His kingdom which will prevail in our world, and for a thousand years all beings on earth will be tremendously blessed under the personal reign of the Lord Jesus Christ.

> Daniel 2:46-49:
> Then the king Nebuchadnezzar fell upon his face, and worshipped Daniel, and commanded that they should offer an oblation and sweet odours unto him.
> The king answered unto Daniel, and said, Of a truth it is, that your God is a God of gods, and a Lord of kings, and a revealer of secrets, seeing thou couldest reveal this secret.

Then the king made Daniel a great man, and gave him many great gifts, and made him ruler over the whole province of Babylon, and chief of the governors over all the wise men of Babylon.

Then Daniel requested of the king, and he set Shadrach, Meshach, and Abednego, over the affairs of the province of Babylon: but Daniel sat in the gate of the king.

DANIEL'S GOD IS GREATEST!

Nebuchadnezzar's subjects often fell on their faces before their leader, but for the king to subject himself to such a humble posture meant that Daniel had indeed gotten through to him. It also appeared that Nebuchadnezzar may have been making some spiritual progress, revealed by his act of contrition, admitting that Daniel's God was the greatest god of all. The king made good on his promise that he would reward the wise one who met the demands of speaking and interpreting his dream, and Daniel was subsequently exalted throughout the realm. But Daniel, always a man of integrity, did not forget his friends, and he requested that the king give them key positions as well. His wish was granted. Daniel continued to be a person of great influence in the king's court by being allowed to sit in the gate of the king — a position of judge, the equivalent of a Supreme Court justice and confidant of the king. Yet Daniel never compromised his standards in that foreign land.

Through it all, Daniel remained faithful to his God, continuing to speak the truth fearlessly, always serving notice to Nebuchadnezzar that God alone, not earthly kings, has the real power. God does not tremble at the sight of monarchs. If anything, He laughs at their rebellion, and in Psalm 2:1-4 — a passage that pictures the battle of Armageddon — we read: "Why do the heathen rage, and the people imagine a vain thing? The kings of the earth set themselves, and the rulers take counsel together, against the Lord, and against his anointed, saying, Let us break their bands asunder, and cast away their cords from us. He that sitteth in the heavens shall laugh: the Lord shall have them in derision."

✠

CHAPTER 5
TWO POPES —
JOHN PAUL II AND GREGORY XVI

This chapter reports the struggles and errors creeping into Catholicism because of the Jesuit Marxist Society of Jesus.

Inside the Vatican, in a special issue published in June-July 2013, ran this fascinating interview:

John Paul II and Liberation Theology[xxxii]
An interview with Professor Rocco Buttiglione, the Polish Pope's philosopher
Inside the Vatican, June/July 2013 issue
by Wlodzimierz Redzioch
John Paul II has gone down in history as the pope who disciplined the liberation theologians of Latin America. You played a key role in this event. Could you please tell us more about it?

Professor Rocco Buttiglione: We have to start from the very first days of John Paul II's pontificate. Before going to Poland the Pope had been to Latin America. Paul VI had promised to attend the Third Latin American Bishops' Conference in Puebla, and John Paul II kept this promise. The Third Bishops' Conference was very important because "rebellious" sociology had developed dramatically in Latin America; this sociology regarded the underdevelopment of the continent as a consequence of the capitalist market. At the time the catchword was Mao's sentence: "Lift yourselves up by your own bootstraps"; underdeveloped countries were exhorted to find a way out of the capitalist market and build up a socialist economy. Liberation theology developed in the wake of this sociology. It all started with Gustavo Gutierrez' book *Liberation Theology*, published in 1968. This book was considered to be the result of Vatican Council II and of the Latin American Bishops' Conference of Medellin.

What is the message of liberation theology?

It considers the Christian message, not in the abstract, but relates it to the daily life and suffering of the Latin American pauper, to his hopes and journey to liberation. Theology is about eternal life, but Christ's message is also an exhortation to solidarity, hence a stimulus to transform this world into a place worth living. There is also a third assumption: Marxism is the starting point of liberation, as conceived in the history of Latin America. It makes it possible for us to understand the world from the point of view of the destitute.

William Bigelow, a columnist for Breitbart.com wrote a very interesting article entitled *Pope Francis: Liberation Theologian?* on April 28, 2013.

In it he relates how those proponents of Liberation Theology feel that after being held back by the previous two Popes, Benedict XVI and John Paul II, their core tenets would be "championed" by Pope Francis.

He quotes Leonardo Boff, a prominent liberation theologian, as saying, "Pope Francis will fix a church 'in ruins.'"[xxxiii]

In a separate article in the *Vatican Insider*, Boff stated that with the election of Pope Francis, "We have come from a dark and very hard winter. Now spring has arrived."[xxxiv]

In his last paragraph, Bigelow points out that the connection between Marxism and Liberation Theology at its core is the belief that salvation is accomplished by the redistribution of wealth to achieve political and economic parity, as opposed to the central Christian idea that salvation comes through grace alone.

The final paragraph in Bigelow's piece shows that Liberation Theology is a clear rejection of Ephesians 2:8-9: "For by grace are ye saved through faith; and that not of yourselves: it is the gift of God: Not of works, lest any man should boast."

For further study, please see Chapter 2 on Liberation Theology.

Pope Benedict XVI's Battle Against Persecution[xxxv]
The Pope retired in February, after committing his life to ending global religious oppression.
By David A. Patten
Newsmax, April 2013

Pope Benedict XVI's decision to step down on Feb. 28 marked the end of an extraordinary papacy that confronted the secular world with a stalwart defense against religious persecution.

As leader of the world's 1.2 billion Catholics, Pope Benedict spoke out against religious persecution in communist countries, advised Christians in the Middle East to weather the Arab Spring, and unmasked secular Western forces coercing churches to participate in anti-life activities.

Many observers expect Benedict's voice to reverberate long after the rumors of intrigue swirling around the circumstances of his resignation fade.

Religious liberty was a theme the Pope presented in his first encyclical, "Deus Caritas Est," and expounded upon in his June 2009 encyclical "Caritas in Veritate."

Warning against any state effort to impose "practical atheism" on its citizens, he declared, "Man is not a lost atom in a random universe: He is God's creature, whom God chose to endow with an immortal soul and whom he has always loved."

To advance that notion, he elevated the status of the Aid to the Church in Need group, a Catholic charity that contributes over $100 million a year in aid to churches facing persecution and hardship. And he returned to the theme in his January 2012 address to visiting U.S. bishops. "It is imperative that the entire Catholic community in the United States come to realize the grave threats to the church's public moral witness presented by a radical secularism which finds increasing expression in the political and cultural spheres," he told the American Catholics.

In furtherance of religious freedom, Benedict repeatedly reached out to Jewish […] leaders. In 2008, he visited Rabbi Arthur Schneier's Park East Synagogue in New York City — the first time a Pope had stepped into a U.S. synagogue.

"He was a voice very much against the tide of relativism and secularism," Schneier, who also accompanied the Pope on his historic visit to the Western Wall in Jerusalem, recalls of his friend. "I think he was sort of a spiritual anchor against the tide that is sweeping Europe and a secular society."

In the World Day of Peace message that Benedict delivered just six weeks before his announcement that he would step down as bishop of Rome, he warned of a growing intolerance toward those who dare to live out their faith in society, stating that "even in countries of long-standing Christian tradition, instances of religious intolerance are becoming more numerous."

Benedict even carried his message of religious freedom to Beirut, Lebanon. During a September 2012 visit, he proclaimed that Muslims and Christians must set aside violence, and offered a word of encouragement for the Syrian refugees driven from their homeland by war and persecution.

"I want to say how much I admire your courage," he told them. "Tell your families and friends back home that the Pope has not forgotten you."

LOVE FOR ISRAEL

Pope's New Book Absolves Jews

In 2011, Pope Benedict published a book, entitled *Jesus of Nazareth — Holy Week: From the Entrance into Jerusalem to the Resurrection*, in which he stated that the Jewish people were not collectively responsible for the death of Jesus. In a review of this book in the April 2011 issue of *Israel Today*, Ryan Jones stated: "Given the Pope's influence over the world's more than 1 billion Catholics, the book has the potential to draw many more Christians into an understanding of the Jews' place in God's plan of redemption."

DEATH THREAT

Perhaps the most important religious development in our time is the rise of Islamist fundamentalism. Benedict courted controversy over Islam with his 2006 speech, 'Faith and Reason,' in Regensburg, Germany. He quoted the 14th-Century Byzantine Emperor Manual II Paleologus saying:

"Show me just what Muhammad brought that was new, and there you will find things only evil and inhuman, such as his command to spread by the sword the faith he preached."[xxxvi]

[These quotes led to death threats against Pope Benedict XVI! —Dr. Van Impe]

As a result, Pope Benedict was caught up in a conflict with Islamists. Aaron Klein of WorldNetDaily interviewed Sheik Abu Saqer, a leader of the Jihadia Salafiya Islamic outreach movement, who stated: "...We did not need the words of the pope in order to understand that this is a

Crusader war against Islam, and it is our holy duty to fight all those who support the pope … the green flag … of Muhammad will soon be raised over the Vatican and all around the world and on the fortresses of those who want to destroy Islam...."[xxxvii]

Pope, Citing Health, Is First in Centuries to Resign[xxxviii]
The Wall Street Journal online, February 12, 2013

Pope Benedict XVI will become the first pontiff in six centuries to resign, marking the end of a transitional papacy that focused more on theological and internal renewal and less on the broader challenges that face the Roman Catholic church at the start of its 21st century of existence.

The pope's surprise announcement paves the way for a successor who will confront anew the task of rebuilding the church's foundations in an increasingly secular and skeptical West while continuing to spread its roots in the rapidly growing emerging world.

Benedict Steps Down[xxxix]
By Robert Moynihan
Inside the Vatican

On February 11, Pope Benedict XVI stunned the world by his announcement — in Latin — that he would step down from his papal office on February 28 at 8 p.m. … Thus began an historic period for the Church, which is still continuing....

Pope Benedict XVI was quoted in *The Wall Street Journal* as saying: "Long ago when I was a Cardinal I realized that the role of the Holy Spirit in the conclave is to prevent us from electing a pope who will completely destroy the church." He was pleading with the Cardinals to spend time in prayer because prophecy teaches that a Pope will arise and destroy Catholicism!

Pope Benedict has been the greatest theologian of the Church in our day.

He edited the new Catholic Catechism while he was Cardinal Ratzinger.

His theology is free from Jesuit Marxist error and his point-by-point listing of verses concerning Christ's return is 100% in line with God's Holy Word and my personal beliefs.

Those within Protestantism who erroneously preach "Preterism" and Replacement Theology need the following information from Pope Benedict XVI in the Catholic Catechism:

Point	Subject
840	The Coming of Messiah.
2816	The Kingdom of God lies ahead of us. In Christ we shall reign.
2817	The petition is "Maranatha," the cry of the Spirit and Bride, meaning "Come Lord Jesus!" Indeed as soon as possible, Lord, may your Kingdom come.
2818	In the Lord's Prayer, "Thy kingdom come" refers primarily to the final coming of the reign of God through Christ's return.
2853	The Spirit and the Church pray: "Come Lord Jesus." Since His coming will deliver us from the evil one.
769	The Church longs for the full coming of the Kingdom, when she will "be united in glory with her King."
1042	The universe itself will be renewed — not re-created.
1047	"The visible universe then is itself destined to be transformed — restored to its original state."
765	The 12 tribes of Israel are the foundation stones of the New Jerusalem.
349	"The eighth day begins the new creation."

The Catholic Encyclopedia (published by Broderich Printers) also promotes the exact message I proclaim globally — the four major Protestant denominations that erroneously teach "Preterism" and blasphemous replacement theology are totally in the dark as to the biblical message of Christ's return.

Page 86   "We have the expectation of a blessed, hope-filled return of the Lord."

Page 110	"Chiliasm [millennialism] was the belief of the early Christians. It consisted of a reign of one thousand years under Christ as taught in the 20th chapter of the book of Revelation [or the Apocalypse]."
Page 142	"We look for the resurrection of the dead and the life of the world to come."
Page 318	"The spiritual Kingdom of God will be restored through the second coming of Christ, called the 'parousia.' It was foretold by Christ" (Mark 13:24).
Page 513	"There is a day when the elect will be united in that Holy city, ablaze with the splendor of God, where the nations will walk in His light" (Revelation 21:32-17).
Page 524	"When Christ shall appear and the glorious resurrection of the dead takes place, the splendor of God will brighten the heavenly city and the Lamb [Christ] will be the lamp or light thereof."
Page 583	"The Transfiguration serves as a sure pledge of Christ's future glory." The Transfiguration pre-figures the everlasting enthronement of Christ in the beginning of His reign.

✠

CHAPTER 6
POPE FRANCIS, ARMAGEDDON,
AND CHRIST'S RETURN

I searched scores of periodicals and releases on the new Pope and discovered numerous articles concerning the Cardinal of Argentina. What I'm about to write are **not my personal opinions or prophetical predictions**, but rather the views of multiple secular and religious leaders. Much of the material reported will startle you as they have me, especially the predictions about this Pope being the one who reigns during Armageddon, as well as the time of Christ's return.

Jesuits Had Past Struggles With Popes[xl]
By José De Córdoba and Ben Kesling
The Wall Street Journal, **March 14, 2013**
Jorge Mario Bergoglio's election as Pope Francis brings new attention to his religious order, the powerful and controversial Society of Jesus, better know as the Jesuits.

Among the Jesuits' defining characteristics are their reputation for rigorous intellectual discussion and their lack of dogmatism. "They are very innovative and tied to reality," says Elio Masferrer, an expert on religion at Mexico's National Institute of Anthropology and History.

The Jesuits are the largest single order in the Catholic Church. Throughout their history, they have wielded power as advisers to monarchs and princes alike. They have also produced notable scientists, educators and missionaries, and have also been at the forefront of social movements.

They were founded by St. Ignatius of Loyola, a Basque soldier who had a vision in 1521 while recuperating after his leg was shattered by a French cannonball. The order was organized on military lines of soldier-priests uniquely at the Pope's orders. Throughout their history, the Jesuits have enjoyed a reputation for their intellectual acuity and have played a leading role in Catholic education. Today, they run more than 100 colleges around the world.

The Jesuits also have a reputation for bold missionary activities. They evangelized much of Asia in the 16th century, acting as emissaries to the emperor of China, among other kingdoms.

In that sense, Francis, the name taken by the new pope, is symbolic. It could refer either to St. Francis of Assisi or the well-known Jesuit, St. Francis Xavier, both missionaries, said Terrence Tilley, chair of the Department of Theology at Fordham University in New York....

Through their almost 500 years of history, the Jesuits have at times had difficult relations with the papacy, which sometimes saw them as rivals.

The Society of Jesus was even dissolved by the papacy in 1773. But the Jesuits managed to survive in Russia and Prussia, whose rulers refused to obey the papal bull, which was eventually rescinded in 1814.

More recently, the Jesuits had a particularly strained relationship with the late Pope John Paul II, during the turbulent decades when someone in the church took a leftward turn and Latin America was a front in the Cold War between the U.S. and the Soviet Union....

Earlier in Mexico, Jesuits were expelled from the conservative business capital of Monterrey by the local bishop who thought they were too close to leftist students. ["Leftist students" were communists. —Dr. Van Impe]

The Jesuits: 'God's Marines'[xli]
Cardinal Jorge Mario Bergoglio has become the first Jesuit pope in Catholic Church history. How will that influence him?
The Week, March 23, 2013

Who are the Jesuits?

Formally called the Society of Jesus, they are the largest single religious order in the Catholic Church. The society was founded in Paris in 1534 by St. Ignatius Loyola, a Basque soldier who discovered his faith while recuperating from a cannonball wound. He and six fellow students at the University of Paris, including St. Francis Xavier, dedicated themselves to serving the pope as missionary soldiers of Christ. The order was originally organized along military lines, under the leadership of a "Father General." Early followers named themselves "The Company of Jesus," and were nicknamed "God's Marines," for their willingness to go anywhere in the world at the pope's command. Pope Paul III recognized them as an order in 1540; today there are over 20,000 Jesuits, including missionaries, teachers, and scholars.

What's their current reputation?

The Jesuits are still viewed within the church as the most liberal of the clerical orders, with a rebellious bent. Because of their missionary work, particularly in Latin America, the Jesuits developed strong sympathy for desperately poor people subjugated by colonial or military governments. In 1974, the society decreed that its mission was the "service of faith, of which the promotion of justice is an absolute requirement." For some priests, this led naturally to a leftist movement called "liberation theology," which champions a revolutionary class struggle pitting the people against the powerful and wealthy. Some Jesuits actually fought alongside communist guerrillas in Guatemala, Honduras, and El Salvador. In 1981, Pope John Paul II, aghast at the political direction the order was taking, overrode the Jesuits' nominee for Father General and appointed a pontifical delegate of his own. That created a split between Jesuits and the Vatican that has not been fully repaired.

Will Francis be a Jesuit pope?

On matters of sexual morality and the role of women, Bergoglio is first and foremost a traditionalist, and not a reformer. In Argentina, he also distanced himself from the liberation theology movement, warning priests it was far too political. Still, Francis shares the Jesuits' intense identification with the poor and powerless; he has called "the unjust distribution of goods" a "social sin that cries out to Heaven." There's little doubt that Bergoglio's Jesuit concern for social inequality will guide the Vatican's direction in coming years. Like other Jesuits, he also has little regard for hierarchy in itself and the trappings of power; he traveled to work in Buenos Aires by public transport. Those who know him say that the new pope will use his position to do what Jesuits have always done — evangelize, especially in the church's new center of gravity in the Southern Hemisphere. The election of a Jesuit as pope sends a powerful message, said Father Kevin O'Brien, a Jesuit who is vice president for mission and ministry at Georgetown University....

[Georgetown is also the school that covered the cross and crucifixion scene at the Pentagon's and the President's request; thus Muslims would not be offended as they viewed Obama's speech. —*Dr. Van Impe*]

KARL MARX

The following heartbreaking story is the reason Pope John Paul II, who, along with President Reagan, brought down the Berlin Wall and much of Communism. Priests throughout South America boast about being Christian Marxist priests or Jesuits. This report is about their head, Karl Marx. Read it and weep.

Rev. Richard Wurmbrand, who was imprisoned for 14 years in Europe for speaking out against communism, wrote a book called *Marx & Satan*, in which he reports that as a young man, Karl Marx professed to be and lived as a Christian. He quotes from Marx's first written work, *The Union of the Faithful with Christ*, which states: "...the union with Christ means a most intimate and vital companionship with Him, keeping Him before our eyes and in our hearts, and being permeated by the highest love, so that we can turn our hearts toward our brothers, united with us through Him, and for whom He had sacrificed himself."

But after high school something changed. He became antireligious. He wrote in *Invocation of One in Despair*:

> "So a god has snatched from me my all
> In the curse and rack of Destiny.
> All his worlds are gone beyond recall!
> Nothing but revenge is left to me!

Then in his poem *The Pale Maiden* he wrote:

> "Thus Heaven I've forfeited,
> I know it full well.
> My soul, once true to God,
> Is chosen for Hell.

WARNING BY BENEDICT REPEATED

Pope Benedict XVI stated: "Long ago when I was a Cardinal I realized that the role of the Holy Spirit in the conclave is to prevent us from electing a pope who will completely destroy the church."

Bishop Sheen also predicted such a day would come.

Historic Choice for Pope[xlii]
Argentine Cardinal Bergoglio becomes Pope Francis
He's first Jesuit, first pontiff from Americas to be chosen
By Nicole Winfield

Associated Press, March 13, 2013

VATICAN CITY — Jorge Bergoglio of Argentina was elected pope Wednesday, becoming the first pontiff from the Americas and the first from outside Europe in more than a millennium. He chose the name Francis, associating himself with the humble 13th-century Italian preacher who lived a life of poverty.

Looking stunned, Francis shyly waved to the crowd of tens of thousands of people who gathered in St. Peter's Square for the announcement, marveling that the cardinals needed to look to "the end of the Earth" to find a bishop of Rome.

In choosing a 76-year-old pope, the cardinals clearly decided that they didn't need a vigorous, young pope who would reign for decades but rather a seasoned, popular and humble pastor who would draw followers to the faith. The cardinal electors overcame deep divisions to select the 266th pontiff in a remarkably fast, five-ballot conclave.

Crowd rushes to hear Pope Francis[xliii]
First public appearance in Rome draws thousands
By Marco R. della Cava

USA TODAY, March 18, 2013

ROME — The full impact of Pope Francis' unexpected rise from little-known cardinal to heralded pontiff was hammered home ... as a crushing capacity crowd jammed St. Peter's Square for a 10-minute prayer....

At Masses in U.S., flock lauds choice of new shepherd[xliv]
By Emma Beck and John Bacon

USA TODAY, March 18,2013

The papal honeymoon of Pope Francis continued ... as Roman Catholics attending Masses across the USA sang praises for the Argentine archbishop picked last week to succeed Pope Benedict XVI.

"It's exciting. He's from a new part of the world. He brings new leadership to the papacy," Ross Brennan, 53, said before Mass at St. Ann's Church in Washington, D.C. "He tries to represent the common man and bring change to the church."

After Mass at St. William Catholic Church in Walled Lake, Mich., Larry Rogers, 75, said Francis "is going to be really, really good. I think he cares about the poor, and I like that."

Francis, until Wednesday known as Archbishop Jorge Mario Bergoglio, has drawn rave reviews for championing the underprivileged in his country and for his own humility.

He lived a simple life as the archbishop of Buenos Aires. After being elected pope, he declined a ride in the Popemobile and later checked himself out of the cardinals' hotel, even paying his own bill. That sounded good to many U.S. Catholics....

American Catholics are hopeful but wary[xlv]
By Cathy Lynn Grossman
USA TODAY, March 13, 2013

U.S. Catholics who dreamed of an American pope got their wish — in a way — on Wednesday.

A South American. It was Cardinal Jorge Bergoglio, archbishop of Buenos Aires, who emerged from the conclave as Pope Francis.

Some U.S. church scholars were thrilled, others cautious, and at least one was critical of another aging pope who may be unwilling or unable to make crucial changes....

Francis also has the administrative talent to bring the creaking, scandal-plagued bureaucracy of the global church, the curia, into order, he says. [University of Notre Dame history professor R. Scott] Appleby called Francis an inspirational "model of personal holiness."

But those in the USA who would like to see major changes such as an end to the tradition of priest celibacy or a fresh look at contraception or a reconsideration of the role of women in priesthood can forget about it. Says Appleby: "No way!"...

New World Pope[xlvi]
An Argentinean Jesuit in the Vatican
By Joseph Bottum
News.com

Pope Francis is the first Jesuit pope and the first non-European pope in 1,200 years.

New World Pope — Restoring Europe's Latin Empire[xlvii]
By Ron Fraser
The Trumpet, May/June 2013

For the first time in history, the pope hails from Latin America. The religious bonds with Europe are long and deep. What will happen when they are revived?

✠
CHAPTER 7
POPE FRANCIS, THE FINAL POPE?

In 2007, the Jesuit's Superior General Father Peter-Hans Kolvenbach became the first-ever Jesuit leader to seek and obtain papal permission to retire from the post. The Jesuits were initially founded with the mission to directly serve the Pontiff, and were even known as the "Pope's cavalry"; however, in the 20th century, a schism developed — in fact, Malachi Martin went so far as to call it a "war" between the papacy and the Jesuits.

The Jesuits felt that the centralized authority of the Church was unacceptable in this day and age. As a result, many Popes, including John Paul II, criticized them for their apparent autonomy. In the January 2008 issue of *Time* magazine, Jeff Israely wrote an article entitled *Jesuits to Elect a New 'Black Pope'* in which he quotes Jesuit Father Jose M. de Vera, the spokesman for the Society of Jesus, as saying: "Yes, we are in the vanguard of the Church … It is not our job to just repeat the catechism, but to do research. Sometimes looking for real truth, you can step over the line...."

According to the Church, they stepped over that line in 2007. So much so that the Vatican doctrinal office issued an official "Notification" to Jon Sobrino, a Spanish Jesuit scholar and proponent of Marxist-inspired liberation theology, for what they considered to be "erroneous … and even dangerous writings."

Then on Saturday, January 19, 2008, Spaniard Aldofo Nicolas was elected as the 30th Superior General of the Society of Jesus, also known as the "black pope."[xlviii]

For centuries, there have been two Popes: one a Jesuit, the other usually a Roman. One wears black clothing and the other white — hence the "black pope." Pope Francis is now a 21st century partaker and leader of both.

Catholic sources such as St. Francis of Assisi, Bishop Sheen, and others have said that there is going to be a final Pope who will defect from the faith. In 1139, in Tuam, Ireland, there was an archbishop by the name of Malachy O'Morgair. Later because he was canonized, he was known as St. Malachy. He had just been to Rome and said that God showed him the future....

In 1138 St. Malachy predicted the remaining succession of Catholic Popes from Pope Celestine II of his day until the final Pope.

According to St. Malachy, there will only be two more Popes to reign after John Paul II, so according to him we have one more after Benedict before Christ returns.

Those among the cardinals, bishops, and priests who deny or ridicule this great prophecy have to contend with five of the greatest Catholic leaders ever. Read on.

The dual report on the final Pope by Malachi Martin is as follows. I'm going all the way back to 1226 and Francis of Assisi. He made a great prediction stating: "There will be an uncanonically elected Pope who will cause a great schism. There will be divers thoughts preached which will cause many, even those in the different orders to doubt, yea, even agree with heretics, which will cause my order to divide. Then there will be universal dissensions and persecutions."

Imagine St. Francis of Assisi hundreds of years ago saying that the last Pope would defect from the Christian faith, and this shocking truth classified in Catholic theology under tradition.

Furthermore, the book *After the Darkness* on page 328 states: "There will come a time of hard trials for the church. Cardinals will be against cardinals and bishops against bishops. Satan will put himself in their midst. In Rome, also there will be big changes. What is rotten will fall, and what will fall must not be maintained. The church will be darkened and the world plunged into confusion."

THE COMPLETE STORY OF MALACHI MARTIN

Who was this tremendous Catholic theologian and author?

Malachi Martin, eminent theologian, expert on the Catholic Church, former Jesuit and professor at the Vatican's Pontifical Biblical Institute, is the author of the national best-sellers *Vatican, The Final Conclave, Hostage to the Devil,* and *The Jesuits.* He was trained in theology at Louvain. There he received his doctorates in Semitic Languages, Archaeology, and Oriental History. He subsequently studied at Oxford and at Hebrew University in Jerusalem. From 1958 to 1964, he served in Rome, where he was a close associate of the renowned Jesuit Cardinal Augustin Bea and Pope John XXIII.

The prophecy of St. Malachy is shocking, and Pope John Paul II believed what was said. In 1139, in Tuam, Ireland, there was an archbishop by the name of Malachy O'Morgair. Later, because he was canonized, he was known as St. Malachy. Now don't confuse this with Malachi Martin we have been discussing because he passed away and is with the Lord. This was St. Malachy in 1139, who had just been to Rome and God showed him what was coming in the future and there would be numerous popes from Pope Cellestine II who would reign for approximately 800 years, and then there would be two more Popes following Pope John Paul II. Now St. Malachy gave poetic descriptions of every one of the Popes, and the shocking thing is, he was right. I totally accept this prophecy because of five outstanding Catholic leaders presented chronologically. First, Francis of Assisi predicted that the final Pope would defect from the faith as already seen. Secondly, Bishop Sheen believed it and promoted it on national television in America.

The False Prophet will have a religion without a cross, a religion without a world to come, a religion to destroy religions. There will be a counterfeit church. Christ's Church will be one, and the False Prophet will create the other. The false church will be worldly, ecumenical, and global. It will be a loose federation of churches and religions forming some type of global association — a world parliament of churches. It will be emptied of all divine content and will be the mystical body of the Antichrist. The mystical body on earth today will have its Judas Iscariot, and he will be the False Prophet. Satan will recruit him from among our bishops.

Thirdly, Malachi Martin in his book, *The Keys of this Blood*, states Pope John Paul II knew from the day he became pope about the apostate defection that was coming, and he knew what the second secret of Fatima was — that there would be this great apostatizing among the clergy, bishops, cardinals, etc." Because Pope John Paul II figured that the prophecy would be true, he did everything possible to keep it from happening in the next choosing of a Pope, when the white smoke would flow. So, before his decease he chose 31 new cardinals. Now there are only 190 cardinals, and 185 had been chosen by Pope John Paul II, five were not. All these men guaranteed when they voted that there would be one more conservative Pope. This would be Pope Benedict XVI, the fourth leader, who would faithfully attempt to keep the defecting Pope from coming to power.

This is why: Pope Benedict XVI stated, "Long ago, when I was a Cardinal I realized that the role of the Holy Spirit in the conclave is to prevent us from electing a pope who will completely destroy the church."

Fourthly, the final Pope would reign who would bring grievous error into the Catholic Church and faith. He would also reign during the Battle of Armageddon. Now please remember the Battle of Armageddon is when the Lord Jesus Christ returns to stop history's most devastating battle (Revelation 11:18 and 16:16). Now let's look at some information from Malachi Martin's book, page 864. As he states: "At that time Roman Catholics will then have the spectacle of a pope validly elected who cuts the entire visible body of the church loose from the traditional unity and the papacy oriented apostolic structure that the church has hitherto always believed and taught was divinely established. The shudder that will shake the Roman Catholic body in that day will be the shudder of its death and agony, for its pains will be from within itself orchestrated by its leaders and its members. No outside enemy will have brought this about. Many will accept the new regime, many will resist. All will be fragmented. There will be no one on earth to hold the fractioning members of the visible Roman Catholic body together as a living compact organization. Men will then be able to ask for the first time in the history of the church, 'Where is the visible body of the church Christ founded?' But there will be none."

✠

CHAPTER 8
THE GLOBAL COLLISION
WITH THE JESUITS

Malachi Martin, a former Jesuit, reveals the apostasy of this once godly order of which Pope Francis is a member. This Christian Marxist order once totally sold out to Christ now promotes a message that is contrary to the main doctrines of Catholicism. Re-read my chapter on the Jesuits, the Society of Jesus.

"A state of war exists between the papacy and the Religious Order of the Jesuits — the Society of Jesus.... And, as with all important events in the Roman Catholic Church, it involves the interests, the lives, and the destinies of ordinary men and women in the millions....

"Almost everything that happens in this war bears directly and immediately on the major dissensions that wrack every nation and people in the world.... It bears right now on the fate in misery or happiness of 350 million people in Latin America. It affects the deeply changing public moral code and national consensus of the American people; ... the security of Israel.... All of these things, separate and unconnected as they may seem, are not only interwoven with one another, but are and will be profoundly influenced by the tides and outcome of the global collision between the papacy and the Society of Jesus."

— From the introduction to *The War*

In *The Jesuits*, Malachi Martin reveals the harrowing behind-the-scenes story of the worldwide Society of Jesus. The leaders and the dupes; the blood and the pathos; the politics, the betrayals, and the humiliations; the unheard-of alliances and compromises. *The Jesuits* tells a true story of today that is changing the face of all our tomorrows.

— *The Wall Street Journal*

WILL POPE FRANCIS WALK IN HIS HERO'S FOOTSTEPS?

Please let me repeat quickly to remind you....

St. Francis of Assisi called together his followers and warned them of the coming troubles: He speaks of (2) end-time characters. A Good Pope. And an Anti-Pope.

1. The time is fast approaching in which there will be great trials and afflictions; perplexities and dissensions, both spiritual and temporal, will abound; the charity of many will grow cold, and the malice of the wicked will increase.

2. The devils will have unusual power, the immaculate purity of our Order, and of others, will be so much obscured that there will be very few Christians who will obey the true Sovereign Pontiff and the Roman Church with loyal hearts and perfect charity. At the time of this tribulation a man ... will be raised to the Pontificate, who, by his cunning, will endeavour to draw many into error and death.

3. Then scandals will be multiplied, OUR Order will be divided, and many others will be entirely destroyed, because they will consent to error instead of opposing it.

4. There will be such diversity of opinions and schisms among the people, the religious and the clergy, that, except those days were shortened, according to the words of the Gospel, even the elect would be led into error, were they not specially guided, amid such great confusion, by the immense mercy of God.

5. Then our Rule and manner of life will be violently opposed by some, and terrible trials will come upon us. Those who are found faithful will receive the crown of life; but woe to those who, trusting solely in their ORDER, shall fall into tepidity, for they will not be able to support the temptations permitted for the proving of the elect.

6. Those who preserve their fervour and adhere to virtue with love and zeal for the truth, will suffer injuries and, persecutions as rebels and schismatics; for their persecutors, urged on by the evil spirits, will say they are rendering a great service to God by destroying such pestilent men from the face of the earth. But the Lord will be the refuge of the afflicted, and will save all who trust in Him. And in order to be like their Head, [Christ] these, the elect, will act with confidence, and by their death will purchase for themselves eternal life; choosing to obey God rather than man, they will fear nothing, and they will prefer to perish rather than consent to falsehood and perfidy.

7. Some preachers will keep silence about the truth, and others will trample it under foot and deny it. Sanctity of life will be held in derision

even by those who outwardly profess it, for in those days Jesus Christ will send them not a true Pastor, but a destroyer."

—*Works of the Seraphic Father St. Francis of Assisi,*
Washbourne, 1882, pp. 248-250

From Bishop Dave Williams, Assemblies of God, U.S.A.:

We were watching a TV show last night with Tom Horn and Cris Putnam....

I totally accept the prophecy of St. Malachy of Ireland who reported on the 113 popes who ruled since Celestine II.

One point that I wondered about was that the final pope would choose the title: Peter Roman or Peter the Roman.

✦ Pope Francis is of Italian descent

✦ Took name after St. Francis of Assisi

✦ Original name of St. Francis before baptism was Pietro (Peter)

✦ St. Francis of Assisi, Italian San Francesco d'Assisi, baptized Giovanni, renamed Francesco, original name was Francesco di Pietro (PETER) di Bernardone[xlix]

Pope Sets in Motion Overhaul of Vatican[l]
by Stacy Meichtry
The Wall Street Journal, April 15, 2013

In his first major move as the new leader of the Roman Catholic Church, Pope Francis on Saturday appointed a panel of cardinals from around the world to advise him in overhauling the Roman Curia, the scandal-plagued administrative body of the Vatican. On Sunday, he followed that up by telling priests to practice what they preach.

The Vatican said eight cardinals — ranging from Cardinal Sean O'Malley of Boston to Cardinal Oswald Gracias of Bombay — will be responsible for drawing up a plan to revise the Curia's constitution. That document defines the roles and reporting lines within Vatican central administration, determining how the pope governs his 1.2 billion-strong flock in matters including doctrine, bishop appointments and Vatican finances.

Sunday during a Mass in Rome, Pope Francis said ordinary Catholics need to "see in our actions what they hear from our lips."

"Inconsistency on the part of pastors and the faithful between what they say and what they do, between word and manner of life, is undermining the church's credibility," he said.

The announcement of the panel marked the opening salvo of a papacy that many cardinals and rank-and-file Catholics expect to introduce sweeping changes.

By taking on the powerful Curia just one month into his pontificate, Pope Francis is steering straight into the eye of the storm. The Catholic Church is beset with problems world-wide that the creaky centuries-old Curia has struggled to face down.

In Latin America, Catholicism's most populous region, the church is running up against competition from newer evangelical ministries that have made inroads with the urban poor. In the West, the church is saddled with a sexual-abuse crisis that had undercut the credibility of church hierarchy.

In the run-up to the conclave that elected Pope Francis, cardinals from around the world plunged into an unusually frank debate over how to fix the Curia. Many church officials believe its powers were too centralized under Pope Benedict XVI. Some cardinals think Vatican cardinals need to set up more transparent channels of communication.

Nearly all of the cardinals advising Pope Francis on the administrative overhaul come from archdioceses far from the insular world of Vatican politics. Only one member comes from inside the Vatican City.

The group, which doesn't have legislative power, is scheduled to meet in October, the Vatican said.

Pope names cardinals to advise on reform[li]
Some have called for Vatican shake-up
By Nicole Winfield
Associated Press, April 14, 2013

VATICAN CITY — Pope Francis named eight cardinals from around the globe, including one from Boston, on Saturday to advise him on running the Catholic Church and reforming the Vatican bureaucracy, marking his first month as pope with a major initiative to reflect the universal nature of the church in key governing decisions.

The advisory panel includes only one current Vatican official. The rest are cardinals from North, Central and South America, Africa, Asia, Europe and Australia.

Many have been outspoken in calling for a shake-up of the Vatican bureaucracy, which was last reformed 25 years ago, while others have tried to clean up the church from sexually abusive priests....

Pope Francis faces many scandals as he steps into the Papacy, including cleaning up the administration and finances of the Church as well as restoring its moral leadership role.

Many saw his predecessor, Pope Benedict XVI, as a great spiritual leader but a poor manager who left the Roman Curia in disarray. Most agree that the Church needs not just an intellectual but an inspiring pastor and manager. In one article, Alvise Armellini, quotes Francesco Clementi, from the University of Perugia, as stating he believes Pope Francis has what it takes: "He has a very strong pastoral profile, he is a simple man who lives simply, but he also has a great expertise of government since he has occupied practically all posts in the Curia...."

✠

CHAPTER 9
POPE FRANCIS AND THE VATICAN
AND GAY LOBBY

POPE BENEDICT'S STAND

"Who is guilty of pedophilia cannot be a priest. We hope that we can do, and we have done and will do in the future, all that is possible to heal this wound."

Pope Francis makes a number of moves that are shocking and unscriptural as far as the Catholic Catechism and the rules of the faith are concerned:

Pope Says 'Gay Lobby' Is at Work In Vatican[lii]
By Stacy Meichtry
The Wall Street Journal, June 12, 2013
A scandal that dogged the Vatican in the weeks leading up to Pope Francis's election re-emerged this week after the pontiff was quoted in a memo from a church group discussing the existence of a "gay lobby" within Vatican ranks....

In March 2012, the British government launched a consultation on same-sex marriage, asking the public whether it should be introduced in England and Wales. The response of Cardinal Keith O'Brien of Edinburgh, Scotland, was immediate and vehement.

He stated that the Catholic Church would strenuously oppose any move to recognize same-sex marriage in Scotland. He further stated that the plans were "an attempt to rewrite human nature" and a "direct attack on marriage and the family."

In a commentary in *The Sunday Telegraph*, he stated that he believes that all children deserve to live with a mother and a father, and that same-sex marriage would "create a society which deliberately chooses to deprive a child of either a mother or a father."[liii]

Cardinal O'Brien was an outspoken opponent of homosexuality;

he called it a "moral degradation," and in 2006 criticized Westminster MPs over the introduction of civil partnerships in the UK. Then in 2011, he stated that Scottish society had failed because it encouraged relationships between people of the same sex. He stated that "same-sex relationships are demonstrably harmful to the medical, emotional, and spiritual wellbeing of those involved...."[liv]

CARDINAL O'BRIEN'S HYPOCRISY

Vatican Orders Disgraced Cardinal to Leave Scotland[lv]
By Nicole Winfield
Associated Press, May 15, 2013
　　The Vatican ordered a disgraced Scottish cardinal to leave Scotland for several months to pray and atone for sexual misconduct, issuing a rare public sanction against a "prince of the church" and the first such punishment meted out by Pope Francis.

　　Cardinal Keith O'Brien resigned as archbishop of St. Andrews and Edinburgh and recused himself from the March conclave that elected Francis pope after a newspaper reported unnamed priests' allegations that he acted inappropriately toward them.

　　O'Brien subsequently acknowledged he had engaged in unspecified sexual misbehavior. He apologized and promised to stay out of the church's public life.

　　On Wednesday, the Vatican said O'Brien, once Britain's highest-ranking Catholic leader, would leave Scotland for several months of "spiritual renewal, prayer and penance."

More immoral reports as vile play is promoted at Notre Dame:

Father Jenkins' "Creative Contextualization"[lvi]
The Catholic World Report, **April 25, 2011**
A look at the fallout from and issues raised by the Notre Dame President's decision to keep *The Vagina Monologues* **on campus**

Pope Francis courts gays:

On Gay Unions, a Pragmatist Before He Was a Pope[lvii]
By Simon Romero and Emily Schmall
New York Times, March 20, 2013

BUENOS AIRES — The very idea was anathema to many of the bishops in the room.

Argentina was on the verge of approving gay marriage, and the Roman Catholic Church was desperate to stop that from happening. It would lead tens of thousands of its followers in protest on the streets of Buenos Aires and publicly condemn the proposed law, a direct threat to church teaching, as the work of the devil.

But behind the scenes, Cardinal Jorge Mario Bergoglio, who led the public charge against the measure, spoke out in a heated meeting of bishops in 2010 and advocated a highly unorthodox solution: that the church in Argentina support the idea of civil unions for gay couples.

The concession inflamed the gathering — and offers a telling insight into the leadership style he may now bring to the papacy.

Few would suggest that Cardinal Bergoglio, now Pope Francis, is anything but a stalwart who fully embraces the church's positions on core social issues. But as he faced one of the most acute tests of his tenure as head of Argentina's church, he showed another side as well, supporters and critics say: that he is a deal maker willing to compromise and court opposing sides in the debate, detractors included.

The approach stands in sharp contrast to his predecessor, Benedict XVI, who spent 25 years as the church's chief doctrinal enforcer before becoming pope, known for an unbending adherence to doctrinal purity. Francis, by comparison, spent decades in the field, responsible for translating such ideals into practice in the real world, sometimes leading to a different approach....

Faced with the near certain passage of the gay marriage bill, Cardinal Bergoglio offered the civil union compromise as the "lesser of two evils," said Sergio Rubin, his authorized biographer. "He wagered on a position of greater dialogue with society."

In the end, though, a majority of the bishops voted to overrule him, his only such loss in his six-year tenure as head of Argentina's bishops' conference. But throughout the contentious political debate, he acted as both the public face of the opposition to the law and as a bridge-builder, sometimes reaching out to his critics.

"He listened to my views with a great deal of respect," said Marcelo Márquez, a gay rights leader and theologian who wrote a tough letter to Cardinal Bergoglio and, to his surprise, received a call from him less than an hour after it was delivered. "He told me that homosexuals need to have recognized rights and that he supported civil unions...."

But others who observed the bishops' private annual assembly in 2010 said that the cardinal was earnestly hoping for compromise on the issue.

"He didn't want the church to take a position of condemning people but rather of respect for their rights like any vulnerable person," said Ms. [Roxana] Alfieri, who sat in on the bishops' 2010 meeting....

While the archbishop's support for civil unions was shared by some of the more liberal bishops in attendance, it was defeated by the majority, reflecting the broad resistance of conservative bishops....

Nearly three years since the passage of the law, more than 1,000 gay and lesbian couples have married in Argentina, and specialized tourism for gay and lesbian travelers has grown here, with about 50 tourist couples also taking advantage of the right to marry.

"This is something Rome cannot forgive, tolerate or allow to advance," Father Alessio wrote.

A BETRAYAL OF OFFICE AND CALLING

The Cardinal of Edinburgh, Scotland, betrays his office and high calling of God for strange flesh. 1,600 priests molested boys, and Pope Francis compromised his holy position as Cardinal of Argentina to promote "same-sex" marriage if performed by civil secular servants. A man of God should obey the rules of his church rather than seek the favor of protestors.

Let's look at God's commands:

Romans 1:21-32:
Because that, when they knew God, they
glorified him not as God, neither were thankful; but
became vain in their imaginations, and their foolish
heart was darkened. Professing themselves to be

wise, they became fools, And changed the glory of the uncorruptible God into an image made like to corruptible man, and to birds, and fourfooted beasts, and creeping things.

Wherefore God also gave them up to uncleanness through the lusts of their own hearts, to dishonour their own bodies between themselves: Who changed the truth of God into a lie, and worshipped and served the creature more than the Creator, who is blessed for ever. Amen.

For this cause God gave them up unto vile affections: for even their women did change the natural use into that which is against nature: And likewise also the men, leaving the natural use of the woman, burned in their lust one toward another; men with men working that which is unseemly, and receiving in themselves that recompence of their error which was meet.

And even as they did not like to retain God in their knowledge, God gave them over to a reprobate mind, to do those things which are not convenient; Being filled with all unrighteousness, fornication, wickedness, covetousness, maliciousness; full of envy, murder, debate, deceit, malignity; whisperers, Backbiters, haters of God, despiteful, proud, boasters, inventors of evil things, disobedient to parents, Without understanding, covenantbreakers, without natural affection, implacable, unmerciful. Who knowing the judgment of God, that they which commit such things are worthy of death, not only do the same, but have pleasure in them that do them.

Jude 1:7-25:

Even as Sodom and Gomorrha, and the cities about them in like manner, giving themselves over to fornication, and going after strange flesh, are set forth for an example, suffering the vengeance of eternal fire.

Likewise also these filthy dreamers defile the flesh, despise dominion, and speak evil of dignities. Yet

Michael the archangel, when contending with the devil he disputed about the body of Moses, durst not bring against him a railing accusation, but said, The Lord rebuke thee. But these speak evil of those things which they know not: but what they know naturally, as brute beasts, in those things they corrupt themselves. Woe unto them! for they have gone in the way of Cain, and ran greedily after the error of Balaam for reward, and perished in the gainsaying of Core. These are spots in your feasts of charity, when they feast with you, feeding themselves without fear: clouds they are without water, carried about of winds; trees whose fruit withereth, without fruit, twice dead, plucked up by the roots; Raging waves of the sea, foaming out their own shame; wandering stars, to whom is reserved the blackness of darkness for ever. And Enoch also, the seventh from Adam, prophesied of these, saying, Behold, the Lord cometh with ten thousands of his saints, To execute judgment upon all, and to convince all that are ungodly among them of all their ungodly deeds which they have ungodly committed, and of all their hard speeches which ungodly sinners have spoken against him. These are murmurers, complainers, walking after their own lusts; and their mouth speaketh great swelling words, having men's persons in admiration because of advantage. But, beloved, remember ye the words which were spoken before of the apostles of our Lord Jesus Christ; How that they told you there should be mockers in the last time, who should walk after their own ungodly lusts. These be they who separate themselves, sensual, having not the Spirit. But ye, beloved, building up yourselves on your most holy faith, praying in the Holy Ghost, Keep yourselves in the love of God, looking for the mercy of our Lord Jesus Christ unto eternal life. And of some have compassion, making a difference: And others save with fear, pulling them out of the fire; hating even the garment spotted by the flesh. Now unto him that is able to keep you from falling, and to present you faultless before the presence of his glory with exceeding joy, To the only wise God our Saviour, be glory and majesty, dominion and power, both now and ever. Amen.

Luke 17: 28-30:
Likewise also as it was in the days of Lot; they did eat, they drank, they bought, they sold, they planted, they builded; But the same day that Lot went out of Sodom it rained fire and brimstone from heaven, and destroyed them all. Even thus shall it be in the day when the Son of man is revealed.

1 Corinthians 6:9-11:
Know ye not that the unrighteous shall not inherit the kingdom of God? Be not deceived: neither fornicators, nor idolaters, nor adulterers, nor effeminate, nor abusers of themselves with mankind, Nor thieves, nor covetous, nor drunkards, nor revilers, nor extortioners, shall inherit the kingdom of God. And such were some of you: but ye are washed, but ye are sanctified, but ye are justified in the name of the Lord Jesus, and by the Spirit of our God.

Galatians 5:19-21:
Now the works of the flesh are manifest, which are these; Adultery, fornication, uncleanness, lasciviousness, Idolatry, witchcraft, hatred, variance, emulations, wrath, strife, seditions, heresies, Envyings, murders, drunkenness, revellings, and such like: of the which I tell you before, as I have also told you in time past, that they which do such things shall not inherit the kingdom of God.

Pope Francis, preach and practice 2 Timothy 4:2-5: Preach the word; be instant in season, out of season; reprove, rebuke, exhort with all longsuffering and doctrine. For the time will come when they will not endure sound doctrine; but after their own lusts shall they heap to themselves teachers, having itching ears; And they shall turn away their ears from the truth, and shall be turned unto fables. But watch thou in all things, endure afflictions, do the work of an evangelist, make full proof of thy ministry. Since God judges sodomy as well as your Catholic scriptures and Catechism, it's time you do your duty as the leader of 1.2 billion Catholics and follow God's Word as both Pope John Paul II and Pope Benedict XVI did in their service for God the Father, God the Son, and God the Holy Spirit, who directed the writing of these powerful verses against sodomy and same-sex marriage — II Peter 1:21.

✝

CHAPTER 10
POPE FRANCIS COMPROMISES WITH ATHEISTS AND MUSLIMS

The truth about Pope Francis's relationship with atheists and Muslims is alarming!

Pope Francis suggests atheists' good deeds gets them to heaven[lviii]
By: Cheryl K. Chumley
Washington Times, **May 24, 2013**

Pope Francis has sparked a religious debate with comments made earlier this week confirming atheists can indeed go to heaven.

Christian teaching generally holds that belief in Jesus, and not good deeds, grants eternal life.

But the pope, in a morning Mass on Wednesday, suggested that belief and faith weren't the biggest factors. He said, CNN reported: "The Lord has redeemed all of us, all of us, with the Blood of Christ — all of us, not just Catholics. Everyone. 'Father, the atheists?' Even the atheists. Everyone. We must meet one another doing good. 'But I don't believe, Father, I am an atheist.' But do good: We will meet one another there."

SALVATION BY WORKS?

The Gospel of Christ is diametrically and completely opposed to salvation by doing good works for eternal life. First, Jesus said in Luke 18:19, "None is good save one, that is God." The Holy Spirit directs Isaiah to dogmatically state in Isaiah 64:6: "We are all as an unclean thing and all our righteousnesses are as filthy rags."

Four hundred times the New Testament tells us that Christ and His blood is the only way of salvation. Romans 1:16 states, "For I am not ashamed of the gospel of Christ: for it is the power of God unto salvation to everyone that believeth; to the Jew first, and also to the Greek." Then in I Corinthians 15:1, Paul proclaims the Gospel, and what it is in verses 3 and 4: "That Christ died for our sins according to the scriptures; and that he was buried, and that he rose again the third day according to the scriptures." God condemns any other way. Galatians 1:7-8 says, "There is not another; but there be some that trouble you, and would pervert the gospel of Christ. But though we, or an angel from heaven, preach any other gospel unto you than that which we have preached unto you, let him be accursed." If you look this up in Webster's Dictionary, you will find the meaning of *accursed* as being under a curse and being fried in the fire.

That's why Ephesians 2:8-9 declares, "For by the grace are ye saved through faith; and that not of yourselves: it is the gift of God: Not of works, lest any man should boast." And Titus 3:5 adds, "Not by works of righteousness which we have done, but according to his mercy he saved us, by the washing of regeneration, and renewing of the Holy Ghost." Romans 4:1-6 settles the unscriptural teaching that doing one's best merits eternal life. "What shall we say then that Abraham our father, as pertaining to the flesh, hath found? For if Abraham were justified by works, he hath whereof to glory; but not before God. For what saith the scriptures? Abraham believed God, and it was counted unto him for righteousness. Now to him that worketh is the reward not reckoned of grace, but of debt. But to him that worketh not, but believeth on him that justifieth the ungodly, his faith is counted for righteousness. Even as David also describeth the blessedness of the man, unto whom God imputeth righteousness, with works."

Doing good to earn salvation is the Christian Jesuit Marxist error, not God's Word.

Concerning atheists, God states in Psalm 14:1-3: "The fool hath said in his heart, There is no God. They are corrupt, they have done abominable works, there is none that doeth good. The Lord looked down from heaven upon the children of men, to see if there were any that did understand, and seek God. They are all gone aside, they are all together become filthy: there is none that doeth good, no, not one."

You're wrong scripturally, Pope Francis. Be careful not to mislead millions seeking salvation.

In one of his first addresses as Pope to foreign ambassadors at the Vatican, Francis called for an intensification of dialogue with Islam and non-believers and condemned the 'spiritual poverty' of the developed world.

He stated: "It is important to intensify dialogue among the various religions and I am thinking particularly of dialogue with Islam...."

He also wanted to "intensify outreach to non-believers so that the differences which divide and hurt us may never prevail, but rather the desire to build true links of friendship...."

REMEMBER THE CRUSADES

Dr. Van Impe answers Pope Francis:

Pope Francis, I'm certain you remember the Crusades. Tens of thousands of Christians finally decided to stop the carnage by defending themselves.

Islam has not changed. Believers in Christ are being slaughtered by Islamists in numerous nations. They have already killed 100,000 of their own in Syria.

It has been said that perhaps the most important religious development in our time is the rise of the Islamist fundamentalists. Benedict courted controversy over Islam with his 2006 speech, "Faith and Reason," in Regensburg, Germany. He quoted the 14th century Byzantine Emperor Manuel II Paleologus, saying:

"Show me just what Muhammad brought that was new, and there you will find things only evil and inhuman, such as his command to spread by the sword the faith he preached."

These quotes led to death threats against Pope Benedict XVI.

....Catholicism is under assault by the forces of jihadist Islam in a band of confrontation that runs across the globe from the west coast of Senegal to the eastern islands of Indonesia.

Christian communities in the Holy Land are under constant, often violent, pressure.

Recently, Pope Benedict was caught up in conflict with Islamists. A leader of the Jihadia Salafiya Islamic outreach movement, Sheik Abu Saqer, responded, "We did not need the words of the pope in order to understand that this is a Crusader war against Islam, and it is our holy duty to fight all those who support the pope ... the green flag of Muhammad will soon be raised over the Vatican ... and around the world and on the fortresses of those who want to destroy Islam."

The first thing that Christians need to understand regarding the Islamic belief about Jesus is that Muslims of course reject the idea that Jesus is the Son of God. My rebuttal from the Word of God follows each point:

✸ Matthew 16:13 -18: "When Jesus came into the coasts of Caesarea Philippi, he asked his disciples, saying, Whom do men say that I the Son of man am? And they said, Some say that thou art John the Baptist: some, Elias; and others, Jeremias, or one of the prophets. He saith unto them, But whom say ye that I am? And Simon Peter answered and said, Thou art the Christ, the Son of the living God. And Jesus answered and said unto him, Blessed art thou, Simon Barjona: for flesh and blood hath not revealed it unto thee, but my Father which is in heaven. And I say also unto thee, That thou art Peter, and upon this rock I will build my church; and the gates of hell shall not prevail against it."

✸ John 3:36: "He that believeth on the Son hath everlasting life: and he that believeth not the Son shall not see life; but the wrath of God abideth on him."

✸ Hebrews 1:8: "But unto the Son he saith, Thy throne, O God, is for ever and ever: a sceptre of righteousness is the sceptre of thy kingdom."

Islam claims Jesus never died on the cross for the sins of mankind.

✸ Colossians 1:20: "And, having made peace through the blood of his cross, by him to reconcile all things unto himself; by him, I say, whether they be things in earth, or things in heaven."

✸ I Corinthians 1:18: "For the preaching of the cross is to them that perish foolishness; but unto us which are saved it is the power of God."

✸ Galatians 6:14: "But God forbid that I should glory, save in the cross of our Lord Jesus Christ, by whom the world is crucified unto me, and I unto the world."

- ✠ Philippians 3:18: "For many walk, of whom I have told you often, and now tell you even weeping, that they are the enemies of the cross of Christ...."

Jesus was not in any way a "Savior"?

- ✠ I John 4:14: "And we have seen and do testify that the Father sent the Son to be the Saviour of the world."
- ✠ Luke 19:10: "For the Son of man is come to seek and to save that which was lost."
- ✠ Titus 2:13: "Looking for that blessed hope, and the glorious appearing of the great God and our Saviour Jesus Christ."

Jesus' return is described as taking place just outside of Damascus.

- ✠ Zechariah 14:4: "And his feet shall stand in that day upon the mount of Olives, which is before Jerusalem on the east, and the mount of Olives shall cleave in the midst thereof toward the east and toward the west, and there shall be a very great valley; and half of the mountain shall remove toward the north, and half of it toward the south."

He returns as the subordinate of the Muslim Messiah, Mahdi.

- ✠ Revelation 19:11,16; 20:4: "And I saw heaven opened, and behold a white horse; and he that sat upon him was called Faithful and True, and in righteousness he doth judge and make war.... And he hath on his vesture and on his thigh a name written, KING OF KINGS, AND LORD OF LORDS.... And I saw thrones, and they sat upon them, and judgment was given unto them: and I saw the souls of them that were beheaded for the witness of Jesus, and for the word of God, and which had not worshipped the beast, neither his image, neither had received his mark upon their foreheads, or in their hands; and they lived and reigned with Christ a thousand years."

✠ Philippians 2:10-11: "That at the name of Jesus every knee should bow, of things in heaven, and things in earth, and things under the earth; And that every tongue should confess that Jesus Christ is Lord, to the glory of God the Father.

Jesus returns as the faithful Muslim. Jesus will rule the Muslims according to the divine law (Sharia). Nonsense — Jesus will rule under the 10 Commandments the Holy Spirit led Moses to write.

✠ Exodus 20:3-17: "Thou shalt have no other gods before me. Thou shalt not make unto thee any graven image, or any likeness of any thing that is in heaven above, or that is in the earth beneath, or that is in the water under the earth. Thou shalt not bow down thyself to them, nor serve them: for I the LORD thy God am a jealous God, visiting the iniquity of the fathers upon the children unto the third and fourth generation of them that hate me; And shewing mercy unto thousands of them that love me, and keep my commandments. Thou shalt not take the name of the LORD thy God in vain; for the LORD will not hold him guiltless that taketh his name in vain. Remember the sabbath day, to keep it holy. Six days shalt thou labour, and do all thy work: But the seventh day is the sabbath of the LORD thy God: in it thou shalt not do any work, thou, nor thy son, nor thy daughter, thy manservant, nor thy maidservant, nor thy cattle, nor thy stranger that is within thy gates: For in six days the LORD made heaven and earth, the sea, and all that in them is, and rested the seventh day: wherefore the LORD blessed the sabbath day, and hallowed it. Honour thy father and thy mother: that thy days may be long upon the land which the LORD thy God giveth thee. Thou shalt not kill. Thou shalt not commit adultery. Thou shalt not steal. Thou shalt not bear false witness against thy neighbour. Thou shalt not covet thy neighbour's house, thou shalt not covet thy neighbour's wife, nor his manservant, nor his maidservant, nor his ox, nor his ass, nor any thing that is thy neighbour's."

Jesus becomes the greatest Muslim evangelist. Ridiculous!

✶ Mark 16:15: "And he [Jesus] said unto them, Go ye into all the world, and preach the gospel to every creature."
✶ Paul declares in I Corinthians 15:1-4: "Moreover, brethren, I declare unto you the gospel which I preached unto you, which also ye have received, and wherein ye stand; By which also ye are saved, if ye keep in memory what I preached unto you, unless ye have believed in vain. For I delivered unto you first of all that which I also received, how that Christ died for our sins according to the scriptures; And that he was buried, and that he rose again the third day according to the scriptures."

Jesus will testify against those who called him Son of God — the Christians. Really? Look at what John wrote:

✶ I John 2:22: "Who is a liar but he that denieth Jesus is the Christ? He is antichrist, that denieth the Father and the Son."

Jesus will abolish Christianity.

✶ Philippians 2:10-11: "That at the name of Jesus every knee should bow, of things in heaven, and things in earth, and things under the earth; and that every tongue should confess that Jesus Christ is Lord, to the glory of God the Father."

NO OLIVE BRANCH

Pope Francis, your olive branch won't last because Sharia law hinders your program. Here's why:

....Sharia is an immutable, compulsory system that Muslims are obliged to install and the world required to adopt, the failure to do so being deemed a damnable offence against Allah. For these ideologues, Sharia is not a private matter. Adherents see the West as an obstacle to be overcome, not a culture and civilization to be embraced, or at least tolerated. It is impossible, they maintain, for alternative legal systems and forms of governments to peacefully coexist with the end-state they seek.

10 Reasons Why Sharia Is Bad for All Societies
By James Alansaman

1. Islam commands offensive and aggressive jihad which is a holy war.
2. Islam orders apostates to be killed.
3. Islam orders death for Muslims and death for non-Muslim critics of Muhammad and the Quran, and even Sharia itself.
4. Islam orders unmarried fornicators to be whipped and adulterers to be stoned.
5. Islam commands all homosexuals to be executed.
6. Islam commands the highway robbers should be crucified or mutilated.
7. Islam commands that a male and female thief must have a hand cut off.
8. Islam allows an injured plaintiff to exact legal revenge, physical eye for physical eye.
9. Islam allows husbands to beat their wives.
10. Islam commands that drinkers and gamblers should be beaten. Sharia ultimately grades society and diminishes freedom.

Furthermore, Pope Francis, this is how the Jesus you preach is pictured as Islam's prophet who executes millions of Jews and Christians when He and "Mahdi," the Islamic Messiah, arrive.

Muhammad Hisham Kabbani
Chairman of the Islamic Supreme Council of America
    ....We see that the Mahdi will lead a world revolution that will institute a "new world order" based on the religion of Islam.
    The Mahdi will offer the religion of Islam to the Jews and Christians; if they accept it they will be spared, otherwise they will be killed.
    And Prophet Jesus will be the executioner under Mahdi and "Islam will be victorious over all the religions."

Not so.

I repeat Philippians 2:10-11, which declares: "That at the name of Jesus every knee should bow, of things in heaven, and things in earth, and things under the earth; And that every tongue should confess that Jesus Christ is Lord, to the glory of God the Father."

Nothing can change this glorious truth of God's Word.

This unusual prophecy about Pope Francis being the final pope is not **MY** prophetic prediction. However, I accept St. Malachy's vision given by the Holy Spirit in 1129. Furthermore, since St. Francis of Assisi, Bishop Sheen, Pope John Paul II, Pope Benedict XVI, and Malachi Martin, the great Catholic instructor at the Vatican, all predict that the final Pope would rule during Armageddon, and also create a great and erroneous doctrinal error within Catholicism, I believe Pope Francis could fulfill this heartbreaking prophecy.

Because of these great leaders, and on the authority of God's Word, I declare to you: Jesus is coming soon. Prepare to meet thy God — Amos 4:12.

BIBLIOGRAPHY

Note: All Web pages active as of October 2013

The Jesuits: The Society of Jesus and the Betrayal of the Roman Catholic Church, Malachi Martin. Reprinted with the permission of Simon & Schuster Publishing Group from THE JESUITS by Malachi Martin. Copyright © 1987 by Malachi Martin Enterprises, LTD. All rights reserved

i   p. 303
ii   305
iii   Ibid.
iv   307
v   309
vi   311
vii   312
viii   313
ix   317
x   132
xi   133
xii   132
xiii   486
xiv   489

The Keys of This Blood: Pope John Paul II Versus Russia and the West for Control of The New World Order, Malachi Martin. Reprinted with the permission of Scribner Publishing Group from the Touchstone edition of THE KEYS OF THIS BLOOD by Malachi Martin. Copyright © 1990 by Malachi Martin. All rights reserved.

xv   p. 674
xvi   75
xvii   76
xviii   74
xix   77
xx   79
xxi   84-85
xxii   256-257
xxiii   259
xxiv   Ibid.
xxv   261
xxvi   Ibid.
xxvii   263
xxviii   656
xxix   654

BIBLIOGRAPHY

Note: All Web pages active as of October 2013

xxx   688

xxxi   684

xxxii John Paul II and Liberation Theology, Interview with Professor Rocco Buttiglione Wlodzimierz Redzioch, Inside the Vatican, June/July 2013 issue Used by permission.

xxxiii http://www.breitbart.com/Big-Peace/2013/04/28/Pope-Francis-Liberation-Theologian

xxxiv http://vaticaninsider.lastampa.it/en/inquiries-and-interviews/detail/articolo/boff-popeel-papa-24413/

xxxv   Pope Benedict XVI's Battle Against Persecution, David A. Patten, Newsmax, April 2013 Copyrighted 2013. NewsMax Media, Inc. 103705:813SH

xxxvi Lecture of the Holy Father Aula Magna of the University or Regensburg, Tuesday 12 September 2006

xxxvii Aaron Klein, WorldNetDaily, September 2006 ttp://www.wnd.com/2006/09/38040/

xxxviii Copyright 2013 Dow Jones & Company, Inc. Pope, Citing Health, Is First in Centuries to Resign, The Wall Street Journal online, February 12, 2013 All Rights Reserved

xxxix Benedict Steps Down, Robert Moynihan, Inside the Vatican Used by permission. All rights reserved.

xl   Copyright 2013 Dow Jones & Company, Inc. All Rights Reserved Jesuits Had Past Struggles With Popes By Jose de Cordoba and Ben Kesling March 14, 2013 http://online.wsj.com/article/SB1000142412788732439280457835882341112691 6.html

xli   The Jesuits: 'God's Marines,' The Week, March 23, 2013 Used by permission. All rights reserved.

xlii   Historic Choice for Pope, Nicole Winfield, Associated Press, March 13, 2013 Used with permission of The Associated Press Copyright ©2013. All rights reserved.

xliii Crowd rushes to hear Pope Francis, Marco R. della Cava, From USA Today, [March 18] © [2013] Gannett- USAToday. All rights reserved. Used by permission and protected by the Copyright Laws of the United States. The printing, copying, redistribution, or retransmission of this Content without express written permission is prohibited

BIBLIOGRAPHY

Note: All Web pages active as of October 2013

xliv At Masses in U.S., flock lauds choice of new shepherd, Emma Beck and John Bacon, From USA Today, [March 18] © [2013] Gannett-USAToday. All rights reserved. Used by permission and protected by the Copyright Laws of the United States. The printing, copying, redistribution, or retransmission of this Content without express written permission is prohibited

xlv American Catholics hopeful by wary, Cathy Lynn Grossman, From USA Today [March14] © [2013] Gannett-USAToday. All rights reserved. Used by permission and protected by the Copyright Laws of the United States. The printing, copying, redistribution, or retransmission of this Content without express written permission is prohibited http://www.usatoday.com/story/news/nation/2013/03/13/pope-francis-us-catholics-reform/1986115/

xlvi New World Pope: An Argentinean Jesuit in the Vatican, Joseph Bottum

xlvii New World Pope – Restoring Europe's Latin Empire http://www.thetrumpet.com/article/10540.20.154.0/europe/restoring-europes-latin-empire

xlviii Jesuits to Elect a New 'Black Pope,' Jeff Israely, TIME, January 2008

xlix https://www.britannica.com/EBchecked/topic/216793/Saint-Francis-of-Assisi

l Copyright 2013 Dow Jones & Company, Inc. All Rights Reserved. Pope Sets in Motion Overhaul of Vatican By Stacy Meichtry April 14, 2013 http://online.wsj.com/article/SB10001424127887324240804578420710330497342.html

li Pope names cardinals to advise on reform, Nicole Winfield, Associated Press, April 14, 2013 Used with permission of The Associated Press Copyright ©2013. All rights reserved.

lii Copyright (c) 2013, Dow Jones & Company, Inc.) World News: Pope Says 'Gay Lobby' Is at Work In Vatican By Stacy Meichtry June 13, 2013 http://stream.wsj.com/story/latest-headlines/SS-2-63399/SS-2-252851/

liii http://www.telegraph.co.uk/comment/9121424/We-cannot-afford-to-indulge-thismadness.html

liv http://www.sconews.co.uk/latest-edition/14858/scotland-fails-homosexual-people/

lv Vatican Orders Disgraced Cardinal to Leave Scotland, Nicole Winfield. Associated Press, May 15, 2013 Used with permission of The Associated Press Copyright ©2013. All rights reserved. http://news.yahoo.com/scottish-cardinal-atone-sexual-misconduct-132541049.html

BIBLIOGRAPHY

Note: All Web pages active as of October 2013

lvi http://www.catholicworldreport.com/Item/397/father_jenkins_creative_ contextualization.aspx#.UgupR23Qe5I

lvii On Gay Unions, a Pragmatist Before He Was a Pope Simon Romero and Emily Schmall From the New York Times [March 13] © [2013] The New York Times. All rights reserved. Used by permission and protected by the Copyright Laws of the United States. The printing, copying, redistribution, or retransmission of this Content without express written permission is prohibited http://www.nytimes. com/2013/03/20/world/americas/pope-francis-old-colleagues-recallpragmatic-streak.html?smid=pl-share&r=0

lviii Pope Francis suggests atheists' good deeds gets them to heaven Cheryl K. Chumley The Washington Times, May 24, 2013 © The Washington Times

NOTES